Teacher's Friend Publications, Inc.

INTERNATIONAL children

a special book of customs, costumes and flags of 22 different nations!

written and illustrated
by

Karen Sevaly

Revised Edition Copyright © 1993

Copyright © 1991
Teacher's Friend Publications, Inc.
All rights reserved.
Printed in the United States of America
Published by Teacher's Friend Publications, Inc.
7407 Orangewood Drive, Riverside, CA 92504

ISBN 0-943263-19-0

Table of Contents

How To Use This Book!

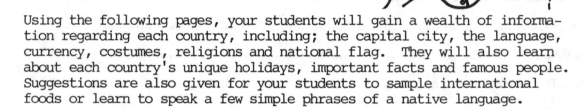

Bon Voyage!

You and your students are about to embark on a fantastic adventure in which you will experience 22 different countries, cultures and customs!

Children love learning about other children and the countries in which they live. They like to know about their similarities as well as their differences.

Using the following pages, your students will gain a wealth of information regarding each country, including; the capital city, the language, currency, costumes, religions and national flag. They will also learn about each country's unique holidays, important facts and famous people. Suggestions are also given for your students to sample international foods or learn to speak a few simple phrases of a native language.

The degree in which your students can use or expand the information given will depend upon their ability and grade level. However, even very young children will love to color the native costumes and learn about the remarkable customs and holidays of each country.

The pages in this book provide a simple starting point to motivating your students in learning more about our world and our neighbors, the "International Children!"

Here are a few suggestions to best utilize the pages in this book:

● Assign each student a specific country to research. Give a copy of the flag and the two children in native costume to each child. Ask them to complete a report noting the facts and points of interest contained in each country's descriptive pages.

● Create an "International Flag" bulletin board by asking each student to use a copy of his or her selected country's flag as a cover for a report. Display the reports on the class bulletin board with the title, "Around the World with the 4th Grade!" or simply "Flags of the World!"

● Give each student a copy of the children in costume appropriate for their assigned country. Ask them to research their country's costumes and color them with suitable colors. Display the international children, with joined hands, circling the classroom. Title the display "It's A Small World!"

● Each month, of the school year, select a country to use as a theme in the classroom. On the first day, read the descriptive page to your students emphasizing the country's unique history, people and traditions. During the first week, display an enlarged copy of the nation's flag and children in costume on the class board. Each day following, write one of the "Interesting Facts" or "Important Holidays" on the chalkboard. Ask students to practice their best penmanship by writing the phrase. Display the best examples. At the close of the month, plan an art or cooking activity appropriate for the given country.

● Each week, of the school year, select an individual country to share with your students. On Fridays, declare the day appropriate for the given country, such as; "Kenya Day" or "Poland Day." Ask students to share interesting facts that they have discovered or researched. Some students may be able to bring in items from home that have been manufactured from the selected nation. They may even like to dress in appropriate costumes. Mark a world map as you circle the globe, country by country.

● Select an area of the classroom to display maps, study books, worksheets and items appropriate for the country being researched. Students can use the area as a study center during free time.

● Contact a local person from the community that was born or has lived in the country being studied. Ask them to come and talk to your students about their country's customs and traditions.

(Note: The Teacher's Friend **MAPS Book: The World and United States** provides a wonderful resource of current, clearly defined, black-line maps for each area and country of the world.)

Country: _____

Capital City: _____
Main Languages: _____
Currency: _____
Area: _____
Population: _____
Main Religions: _____
Government: _____
People: _____
Flag: _____
_____
_____

Interesting Information: _____
_____
_____
_____
_____
_____
_____
_____
_____
_____
_____
_____
_____

Scotland

Capital City: Edinburgh

Main Languages: English and Gaelic

Currency: Pound Sterling

Area: 30,418 sq. mi. (78,783 sq. km.)

Population: 5,146,000

Main Religion: Christian

Government: Constitutional Monarchy (Part of the Kingdom of Great Britain and Northern Ireland.)

People: Scots

Flag: The "Union Jack" is a combination of three flags, the English flag, the Scottish flag and the Irish flag.

The united countries of England, Wales, Northern Ireland and Scotland make up a larger country; The United Kingdom of Great Britain and Northern Ireland.

Long ago, before the great families and clans united, most of the people lived in the highlands. Their rulers lived in castles but the common people lived in small villages with sod huts. The entire area was besieged by various invaders throughout its history including the Romans, Saxons and Angles. Fighting with England was stopped in 1702, when both Scotland and England united to form Great Britain.

The rocky northern highlands take up about one half of the land. Here are found the forested valleys and moors of purple heather. The remainder of the land is used for farming and for grazing cattle and sheep. Oats are the primary crop grown. Between the highlands and the uplands lies a narrow area of fertile lowlands. This is where three-fourths of the people live.

Edinburgh, the capital city and Glasgow, are both home to some of the oldest universities in the world. Edinburgh is an ancient city with age-old ruins and castles. An old castle, "Holyrood" welcomes the Queen of England, on occasion. There is also a "New Town" part of the city with modern shops and homes.

The Scottish "Clans," (a group of family members trained to protect their rights and property) are long gone. But the wonderful customs and traditions of the clans have remained. The Gaelic speaking clansmen gave us bagpipe music, the Scottish fling and plaid kilts. The various colors of the tartan plaids note the family clans.

Interesting Facts:

- The legendary "Loch Ness Monster" lives in Loch Ness Lake in northern Scotland.

- The "thistle" is the national flower of Scotland.

- The ocean liner, "Queen Elizabeth," was built near Glasgow, Scotland.

- The Scots eat salt on their oatmeal instead of sugar.

Important Holidays:

- "Guy Fawkes Day" is celebrated throughout Great Britain on November 5th. In 1605, soldiers of King James I discovered a conspiracy, led by Guy Fawkes, to blow up the House of Parliament. Today, children make effigies of Guy and burn him in a ceremonial bonfire.

- September 6th, all Scots gather for the "Braemar Highland Gathering." Dancers, athletes and bagpipe players all wear their tartan plaid kilts. A contest is held to determine the hardiest of men. They toss a "caber," or long pole, weighing 120 pounds as far as they can.

- On November 30th, Scots celebrate the "Feast of St. Andrew," Scotland's patron saint. On this joyous day an unusual dish is featured called "haggis." This is a pudding made of the heart and organs of a sheep. After the feast, everyone joins in singing favorite songs by the poet Robert Burns.

Famous People:

- Sir Walter Scott, Scottish author of <u>Ivanhoe</u>, was born in 1771.

- Robert Louis Stevenson, Scottish poet and novelist, (<u>Treasure Island</u> and <u>A Child's Garden of Verses</u>) was born in 1850.

- A Scot named Alexander Fleming, discovered penicillin in 1928.

- The Scotsman, James Watt, discovered the unit of power described as "the time rate of energy delivery" or "watt."

Some Things To Do:

- Serve an afternoon "English Tea" for your students, complete with "scones."

- Hold your own "Highland Gathering" by conducting a throwing competition. (Perhaps a softball throwing contest.)

- Ask your students to find out the meaning to these Scottish terms; kilt, clan, gaelic and tartan.

The Flag of the United Kingdom

Scotland

Scotland

Ireland

Capital City: Dublin

Main Languages: English and Gaelic

Currency: Irish Pound

Area: 27,135 sq. mi. (70,280 sq. km.)

Population: 3,535,000

Main Religion: Christian

Government: Republic

People: Irish

Flag: The Irish flag is green, white and orange-red. The green stands for the land, white for peace and orange-red for King William III.

Many people call Ireland the "Emerald Isle" because of the spectacular green of its valleys and rolling hills. This luscious green comes from the abundant rainfall and mineral-rich limestone soil.

To visitors, Ireland seems like a land of enchantment with stories of leprechauns and elves and much song, dance and merrymaking. Thatched roof cottages, winding country roads and "haunted" ruins, lend to the charm of the country.

But, Ireland is actually a very poor country. There is little industry and not enough jobs for its people. During the Great Potato Famine of 1840, thousands fled Ireland to seek opportunities in other lands. Many of these people settled in Canada and the United States.

Saint Patrick's Day is celebrated each March 17th in honor of Ireland's patron saint, Saint Patrick. Patrick was a great teacher and taught many Irish to read and write, along with the study of Christianity. It is believed that he was responsible for bringing the small shamrock plant to Ireland. He often used the shamrock in his sermons to illustrate the message of the holy trinity. On his day, many people celebrate by wearing a shamrock, Ireland's national flower.

Ireland is a country divided. In 1920, the Protestant counties of Northern Ireland split off from the rest of the country to stay under British rule. The rest of Ireland, known as the Irish Republic, was granted independence from England in 1949. Today, much fighting takes place in Northern Ireland. Many wish to be independent of the British monarchy.

Interesting Facts:

● Peat bogs cover almost one-sixth of Irish land. The Irish cut the peat into chunks and burn it as fuel for stoves and fireplaces.

● There are two national sports in Ireland, Hurling and Gaelic Football. The first is similar to field hockey and the second resembles soccer.

● Before 1949, the Irish Republic was known by the name of "Eire."

● The first sweetened carbonated drink was ginger ale. It was invented by the Irishman, Dr. Cantrall, in 1850.

● The Blarney Stone is said to give great powers of persuasion to anyone who kisses it. It's located near Blarney Castle at County Cork.

Important Holidays:

● Ireland is the only country in which Halloween or All Hallow's Eve is a national holiday. It is celebrated on the 31st of October. In the 1840's, the Irish immigrants brought their Halloween customs to North America including the carving of jack-o'-lanterns.

● October 6th, the anniversary of the death of Irish nationalist leader, Charles Stewart Parnell, is observed throughout Ireland. The day is called "Ivy Day" because everyone wears a sprig of ivy on their lapel in rememberance.

● On December 26th, the Day of the Wren, takes place in Ireland. Masked party-goers and musicians go door to door and ask for money. Much singing and dancing follow at large parties.

Famous People:

● George Bernard Shaw, Irish playright, was born in 1856.

● William Butler Yeats, Irish poet and essayist, was born in 1865.

● James Joyce, Irish novelist, was born in 1882.

● Charles Stewart Parnell, Irish patriot and statesman, was born in 1846. His leadership led the fight for Irish independence from Britain

Some Things To Do:

● Declare March 17th, St. Patrick's Day, "Green Day" and have your students come dressed accordingly.

● Make potato prints in honor of Ireland's most important crop.

● Ask students to write creative stories about Ireland's legendary leprechauns.

● Prepare Irish stew and scones in the classroom. Students can each be responsible for supplying the ingredients.

Ireland

Ireland

The Flag of Ireland

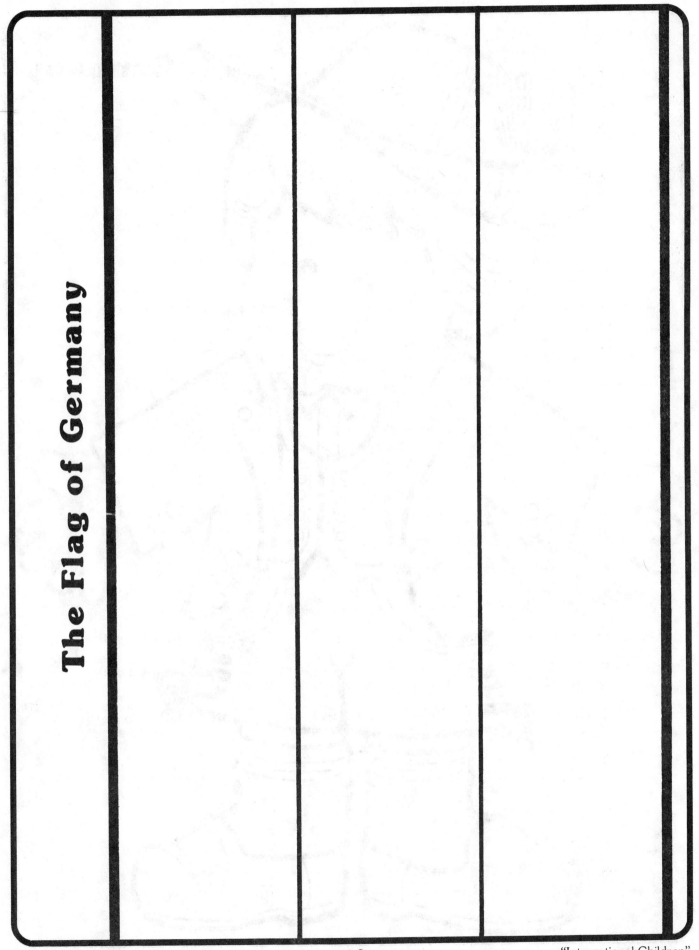

The Flag of Germany

Germany

Germany

Sweden

Capital City: Stockholm

Main Languages: Swedish, Finnish and Lapp

Currency: Swedish Krona

Area: 173,649 sq. mi. (449,750 sq. km.)

Population: 8,345,000

Main Religion: Christian

Government: Constitutional Monarchy

People: Swedes

Flag: The cross on the Swedish flag dates back to 1533. The gold color on bright blue represents the gold crowns of the monarchy.

In the late 1800's, Sweden was a poor nation. Nearly one-fifth of the people immigrated to the United States to seek their fortunes. Today, Sweden is one of the wealthiest countries in Europe with productive farms, huge industries and hydroelectric power plants.

The unusual shape of the entire Scandinavian peninsula was carved by glaciers during the Ice Age. About 10,000 B.C., the first inhabitants came to live in the southern regions. Vikings occupied this area about a thousand years ago. These "Northmen" or "Norsemen" are the ancestors of the Swedes, Norwegians and Danes. Vikings were hearty warriors. They traveled the oceans of the world long before the explorers of Europe. Leif Erikson is believed to have reached North America hundreds of years before Columbus.

Due to the mountains, the winds of the Atlantic Ocean cannot bring the warm air to Sweden as they do to it's neighbor Norway. In the winter, the harbors on the east coast are frozen over. Because of this, fishing industries are not as successful as the active fisheries on the west coast.

There is, however, much fertile farm and forest land in Sweden. Here crops of oats, potatoes and wheat grow abundantly and help supply the numerous dairy farms.

The northern half of Sweden is called "Norrland." Here, Lapp countrymen raise herds of reindeer in a snowbound wilderness. The Lapps live also in Norway and Finland.

Stockholm, Sweden's capital, is a beautiful city built partially on islands. It has been called a model city because of its blend of handsome new highrises and restored ancient buildings. Among its historical buildings is its famous Town Hall.

Sweden is known for its liberal social programs. About one-third of its budget is spent on free education (including college tuition,) free medical care, special allowances for large families and generous pensions for the needy and the elderly.

Interesting Facts:

- Sweden has one of the highest life expectancies at an average of 74.2 years.

- In 1200 A.D., Swedes used skis in combat for the first time in the Battle of Oslo, Norway.

- Ice breakers are used to keep Stockholm's harbors open during the winter months.

- Nobel prizes are awarded annually in Sweden to persons or institutions for outstanding contributions in the fields of physics, chemistry, medicine, literature, economics and international peace.

Important Holidays:

- On December 13th, St. Lucia Day, the eldest daughter of the family rises early in the morning and dresses in a white robe and red sash. Wearing a crown of lit candles, she serves coffee and saffron buns to her parents and other adults.

- St. Knut's Day, January 13th, celebrates the last day of the yuletide season declared by King Knut of Sweden over nine centuries ago. On this day, people celebrate by having a party and taking the decorations off the Christmas tree. Children get to eat the cookie ornaments.

- The Midsommar or "Midsummer" Festival is celebrated on the longest day of the year. On this day, nearly every town decorates it's own maypole and people dressed in costume dance around it. Since the sun sets for only a few minutes on this day, the festivities can last all night.

Famous People:

- Alfred Bernhard Nobel, born in 1833, was a Swedish chemist, inventor and philanthropist. In his will he provided a fund to establish annual prizes for outstanding merit.

- The Swedish astronomer, Anders Celsius, developed the Celsius scale thermometer in 1742.

- Swedish author, Astrid Lindgren, wrote the "Pippi Longstocking" books.

Some Things To Do:

- Teach your students these Swedish phrases: "God dag" (Hello,) "Adjo" (Goodbye) and "Tack" (Thank you.)

- On December 13th, have each girl in class make her own St. Lucia crown. Boys could make Viking helmets.

- Have a Swedish "smorgasbord" in your classroom by having each child bring a special dish or treat.

Sweden

Sweden

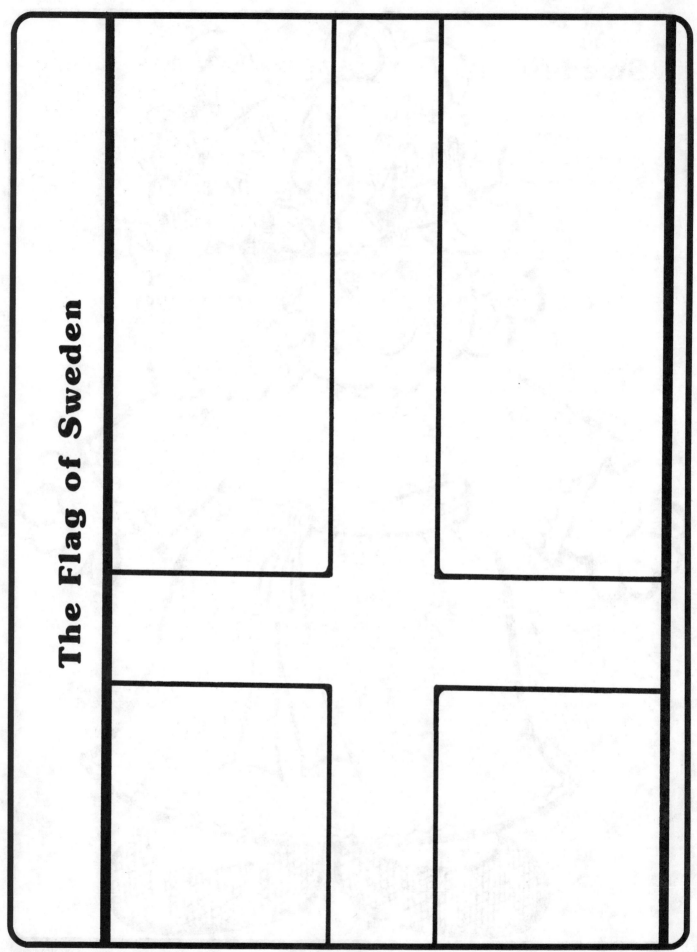

The Flag of Sweden

Poland

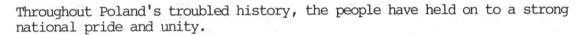

Capital City: Warsaw

Main Language: Polish

Currency: Zloty

Area: 120,726 sq. mi. (312,680 sq. km.)

Population: 37,727,000

Main Religion: Christian

Government: Parliamentary Democracy

People: Poles

Flag: The Polish flag is white on the top half and red on the bottom half.

Throughout Poland's troubled history, the people have held on to a strong national pride and unity.

Before Christ, the western Slavs were the first people to settle the fertile valleys of present-day Poland. In 966 A.D., the Slavs converted to Catholicism and the official state of Poland was born. During the 1700's Polish life declined and the country was divided between Russia, Austria and Prussia. It was not until after World War I that Poland was again given independence. Only twenty years passed when World War II brought the Poles into another great disaster. The Polish Jews suffered mass murder at the hands of Nazi soldiers in established concentration camps. At the close of the war, Poland remained under Soviet rule.

Today, most of the people of Poland live in large cities where they work in state operated factories and refineries. Coal and grain barges move along the Oder and Vistula rivers to the seaports of Gdansk and Szczecin. Here, huge ships and freighters are both built and loaded with goods to be shipped to other countries.

Most of Poland is low and flat, ideal for growing potatoes, rye, oats and sugar beets. Most of the independent farms are quite small, however, and farmers make a poor living. The farmers of southern Poland, the Polandians, "dwellers of the fields," still cut wheat and dig potatoes by hand. In the hills of the High Tatra, mountain men or "gorals" can be found herding sheep and playing an instrument similar to a bag pipe.

Slowly, the Poles are rebuilding their wonderful country. Since the destruction of the last world war, Warsaw, the capital city, has built many new and modern buildings. They stand on the ancient ruins of the past. Visitors, though, can still find beautifully restored palaces and ancient marketplaces at the historic Old Town district of Warsaw.

Interesting Facts:

- "Polska" or Poland comes from the ancient Slavic tribe known as Polanie (field or plain dweller.)

- The Baltic Sea, at the northern coasts of Poland, often freezes in the winter stopping all business in the seaports.

- More than 50% of all medical college graduates, in Poland, are women.

Important Holidays:

- Sometime after Christmas, when the snow is especially deep, friends take horse-drawn sleighs to the "Kulig," a winter sleigh party. When they reach a suitable place in the forest, a fire is made and a hearty supper prepared. Afterwards, they sing and dance around the fire.

- On March 23rd, the older people of Poland make a "Marzenna" doll out of straw and dress her in rags and ribbons. The doll represents the cold, harsh winter months. During the celebrations they carry her to the river and throw her in, singing and dancing all the way. Everyone is joyous over the coming of spring!

- Easter is an important holiday to the Poles. The favorite tradition is to paint beautiful designs with special meanings on Easter eggs. Some areas even have "egg-breaking" contests (hard-boiled, of course!) The owner of the egg which remains unbroken is declared the winner.

Famous People:

- Nicholas Copernicus discovered the radical theory that the earth revolved around the sun. He was born in 1473.

- Marie Curie, Polish-English chemist and physicist, co-discovered radium. She was born in 1867.

- Polish composer, Frederick Chopin, pianist and composer was born in 1810.

- In 1978, Pope John Paul II was declared the first non-Italian cardinal elected Pope in 456 years.

Some Things To Do:

- Teach your students a Polish folk dance (polka.)

- Find pictures of beautifully decorated Easter eggs and ask your students to make similar designs using colored markers.

- Have your students learn these Polish phrases: "Dubryden" (Hello,) "Do Widzenia" (Goodbye) and "Dziekuje" (Thank you.)

- Make a "Marzenna" doll and have your own spring celebration.

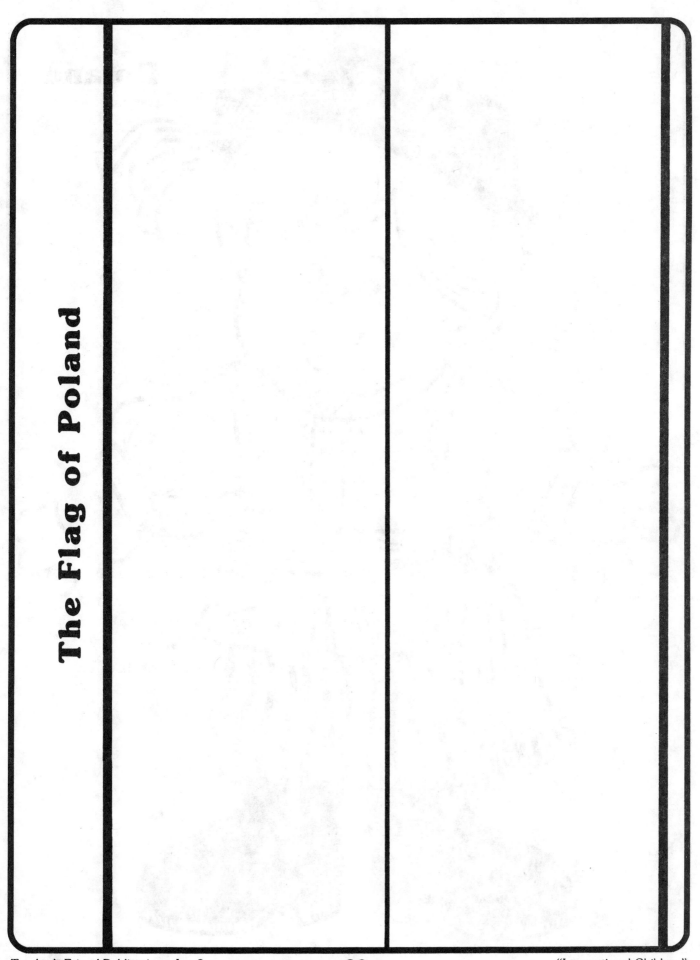

The Flag of Poland

Poland

Poland

France

Capital City: Paris

Main Language: French

Currency: French Franc

Area: 211,207 sq. mi. (547,026 sq. km.)

Population: 52,656,000

Main Religion: Christian

Government: Republic

People: French

Flag: The red, white and blue of the French flag
have inspired many nations to use the same
colors as a symbol of liberty.

The French call their country "la belle, la douce—the beautiful, the
sweet." The land has been blessed with fertile soil, 2,000 miles of
coastline and majestic French Alps.

Farming is an important resource in France. Many areas, such as Cham-
pagne and Burgundy are famous for their world-renowned wines. In the
warm south, crops such as olives, peaches and artichokes grow abundantly.
France is also known for its more than 300 kinds of cheese made from
both goats and cows milk.

The captial city, Paris, is the nation's hub. Each year, thousands of visitors flock to the city to be dazzled by her magnificent parks, boulevards,
monuments and museums. It is indeed a breathtaking city divided in half
by the Seine River. A sixth of France's population lives in and around
Paris.

France once had colonies in various parts of the world, with many in
Africa. These nations are now all independent. The island of Corsica
and several other small islands are still part of France.

The history of Europe can be experienced throughout the French countryside. In ancient times, France was called Gaul. The Romans conquered
Gaul over 2,000 years ago. Evidence of Roman ruins, roads and aqueducts
can still be seen today. After about 500 years of Roman rule, the northern people called "Francs" conquered the area. This is where the name
"France" originated. The king of the Franks was Charlemagne.

Not long after the American Revolution, a French Revolution declared
France a republic. But, soon after, Napoleon made himself emperor of
France. He built elaborate monuments depicting his victories in battle
and his love for the arts.

Today, you can see the evidence of France's history everywhere. The arc
de Triomphe, Chartes Cathedral, the chateaus of the Loire Valley, the
Eiffel Tower, as well as the small fishing villages of Normandy, are a
must for anyone visiting France.

Interesting Facts:

● France is the largest country of western Europe.

● The Eiffel Tower, in Paris, was built for the World's Fair of 1889. It stands 984 feet tall. At the time it was built it was the tallest man-made structure on earth.

● In 1940, near Lascaux, France, four boys went hunting and suddenly lost their dog. They found him barking from a hole in the ground that was part of a huge cave. In the cave they found paintings of animals made by cavemen more than 15,000 years ago.

● The first bicycle was built by a Frenchman, Comte de Sirvac, in 1791.

● Louis Pasteur, a French chemist, was the first to rid milk of harmful bacteria by pasteurization, in 1864.

Important Holidays:

● Bastille Day, July 14, marks the beginning of the French Revolution. Today, it is a national holiday with an elaborate military parade and fireworks.

● In July each year, the Tour de France takes place with thousands of cyclists racing a 2,500 mile course across France. The entire race lasts about three weeks.

● A national French holiday, May 30, in honor of Joan of Arc, is one of the most important French holidays. At the age of 17, she helped bring victory to France and end the Hundred Years' War with England.

Famous People:

● Louis Braille, a French inventor, developed a reading system for the blind. He was born in 1809.

● Jacques Cousteau, French oceanographer, was born in 1910.

● Napoleon Bonaparte, self-proclaimed Emperor of France, was born in 1769.

● Claude Monet, French impressionist artist, was born in 1840.

Some Things To Do:

● Let your students sample some French bread and various French cheeses.

● Stage your own Tour de France.

● Ask your students to draw a picture of one of France's historical monuments, such as; the Eiffel Tower.

● Have your students learn these three phrases: "Bon Jour" (Hello,) "Au revoir" (Goodbye) and "Merci" (Thank you.)

France

France

The Flag of France

Italy

Capital City: Rome

Main Language: Italian

Currency: Italian Lire

Area: 116,305 sq. mi. (301,230 sq. km.)

Population: 57,351,000

Main Religion: Christian

Government: Republic

People: Italians

Flag: The colors of the Italian flag, (green, white and red) are said to represent the virtues of "Faith, Hope and Charity."

The peninsula of Italy resembles a boot kicking the island of Sicily. Its odd shape is caused by a long range of mountains called the Apennines and the beautiful blue waters of the Mediterranean.

Most of the people of Italy live in major cities. Rome, on the Tiber River, is one of the oldest cities in the world. Over 2,000 years ago, Rome was the capital of a vast empire that included all of the land bordering the Mediterranean. The ancient Romans were great architects and builders. Several centuries later, the Roman Empire fell.

During the period of 1300 to 1500 A.D., Italy again flourished. The cities of Italy produced great craftsmen of fine fabrics, glass, jewelry and leather. Italian sculptors, painters, architects, scholars, composers and writers became famous. At this time, the area was divided into many small city-states. It was not until 1870, that Italy was united into one country. After World War II, the Republic of Italy was declared which included both Sicily and Sardinia.

Today, Rome is not only the capital city but the center of transportation and commerce. Here, modern hotels and office buildings stand side-by-side with ancient Roman ruins.

Vatican City, actually the smallest country in Europe, is contained within the city of Rome. The Pope, head of the Roman Catholic Church, resides in Vatican City. His palace and St. Peter's Basilica can be found there.

Each Italian city has its own unique characteristics. Naples is a chief port with a scenic view of famous Mount Vesuvius. Genoa and Milan are huge industrial centers. Florence and Venice offer fantastic attractions of beautiful architecture and works of art.

Interesting Facts:

- The Appian Way is the oldest paved road still in use today. It was built in 312 B.C.

- The Colosseum in Rome is a giant open theatre large enough to seat thousands of spectators. It was completed in 80 A.D.

- Venice is probably the most unique city in Europe. There are no streets in Venice, only canals. People travel by taxi-boats called "gondolas."

- The Tower of Pisa is perhaps the most unusual tower in the world. During construction, the ground beneath began to sink causing it to lean. Today, it leans almost ten feet to one side and will eventually fall over.

Important Holidays:

- On January 5th, on the eve of Epiphany, a fair of toys, candies and presents takes place in Rome at the beautiful Bernini Fountains.

- On January 6th, during the Epiphany Festival, "Befana," a friendly witch, bestows gifts of toys and sweets to Italian children who have been good. Bad boys and girls get lumps of coal.

- April 21st marks the national celebration of the founding of Rome in 753 B.C.

- Mount Vesuvius Day, August 24th, commemorates the anniversary of the eruption of Mount Vesuvius, an active volcano in southern Italy, which destroyed the city of Pompeii in 79 A.D.

- Republic Day is June 2nd and honors the day Italy became a republic and gave up monarchy rule.

Famous People:

- Julius Caesar, great Italian general and statesman, was born in 100 B.C. He laid the foundation for the great Roman Empire.

- Leonardo da Vinci, Italian artist, scientist and inventor, was born in 1452.

- Christopher Columbus, Italian explorer, set sail from Spain on his first voyage to the New World in 1492.

- Galileo Balilei, Italian astronomer and physicist, was born in 1564.

- An Italian, Guglielmo Marconi, invented the wireless telegraph in 1895.

Some Things To Do:

- Write the Roman numerals on the class chalkboard and ask students to convert a few simple math problems using the numerals.

- Teach your students these three Italian phrases: "Bon giorno" (Hello,) "Addio" (Goodbye) and "Grazie" (Thank you.)

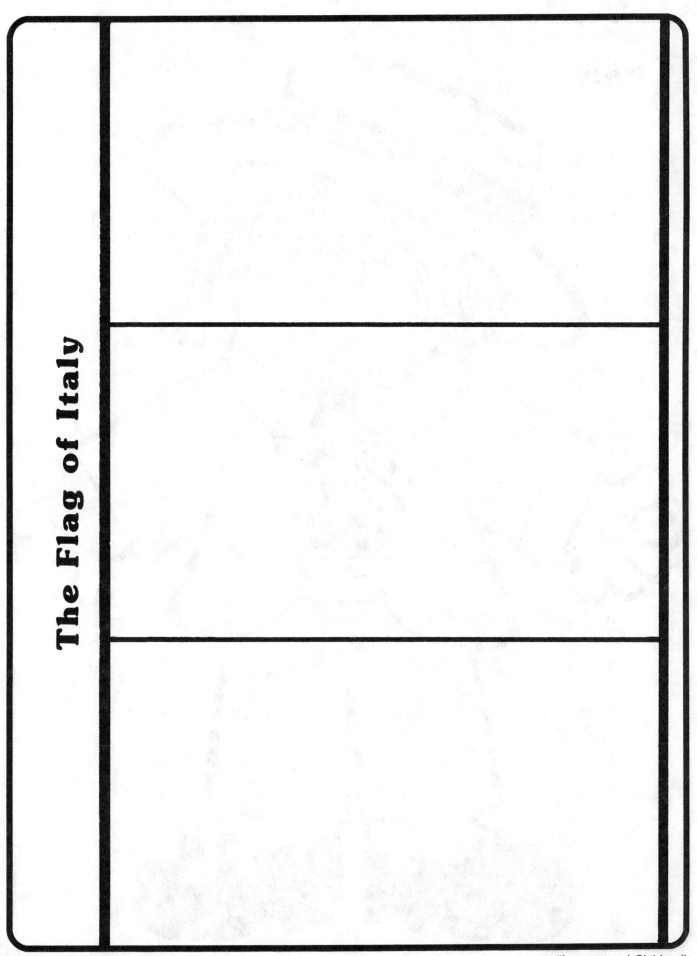

The Flag of Italy

Italy

The Netherlands

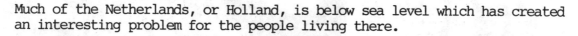

Capital City: Amsterdam

Main Language: Dutch

Currency: Guilder

Area: 14,405 sq. mi. (37,310 sq. km.)

Population: 14,642,000

Main Religion: Christian

Government: Constitutional Monarchy

People: Dutch or Netherlanders

Flag: The official colors of the Dutch flag are red vermilion and cobalt blue. An orange pennant is often flown with the flag to signify the Royal Family of Orange.

Much of the Netherlands, or Holland, is below sea level which has created an interesting problem for the people living there.

Long ago, most of the area consisted of swamps and small lakes. Islands provided homes for small fishing villages. About one thousand years ago, the Dutch began building dikes, or sea walls, along the coastal sand dunes. They also drained the water into canals and rivers, reclaiming the land from the North Sea. These sections of reclaimed land are called "polders." The pumps used to drain the water were run by windmill power. This new land quickly prospered into fertile farmland where wheat, potatoes and tulips now grow. Today, the Dutch continue to push back the sea. About twelve square miles of new land each year is converted into new towns and farmland.

In Amsterdam, the capital city, homes and buildings are built on wooden posts because of the waterlogged soil. A maze of canals run in half circles around the beautiful city. Thousands of tourists a year come to ride the canal boats, visit the fine art museums and view the spectacular tulip fields.

Farming is one of Holland's most important industries. The entire area is famous for its wonderful cheeses and exportation of flower bulbs. Manufacturing is also vital to the country's economy. There are steel mills, shipyards and textile mills, not to mention diamond cutting and the manufacturing of Delft blue china.

The Hague is the seat of government for the Netherlands. The queen opens Parliament there each September. It is also home to the World Court where cases involving international laws and treaties are heard.

Rotterdam is the largest seaport in the world and is the shipping link to many large cities in Europe. It handles fleets of supertankers bringing oil to Europe and cargo ships exporting goods to other countries.

Interesting Facts:

● Netherlands means "the low lands."

● The legend of the Dutch boy using his finger to plug a dike was a fictional story created by Mary Mapes Dodge. However, there is a statue honoring the youngster in Spaarnadan, Holland.

● There are more bicycles per capita in the Netherlands than anywhere else in the world.

● 60% of the Dutch population live on land that has been reclaimed from the sea.

Important Holidays:

● On Vlaggetjesdag or "Flag Day," May 27th, the fishermen in Dutch villages decorate their boats with streamers and flags and head out to sea for their first trip of the year.

● "St. Nicholas Day" is celebrated on December 5th. "Sinterklaas" arrives by steamboat dressed in a bishop's robe with his helpers, "Zwarte Piets" (Black Peters.) That evening families exchange gifts and children leave carrots and hay in their shoes for the Saint's horse. The next morning they receive candies if they have been good!

● "Prinsjesdag," the third Tuesday of September, marks the official opening of Parliament in The Hague. On this day, the queen of the Netherlands rides in a golden coach to the Hall of Knights for the annual celebration.

● January 22nd marks the day of "Elfstedentocht." When the ice is thick enough on the canals, thousands of skaters race a 124 mile course connecting eleven cities in Holland.

Famous People:

● Henry Hudson, English navigator, claimed Manhattan Island for the Netherlands in 1609.

● Anton van Leeuwenhoek, Dutch naturalist and "Father of the Microscope" was born in 1632.

● Famous Dutch artist, Vincent Van Gogh, was born in 1853.

Some Things To Do:

● Teach your students these Dutch phrases; "Goed dag" (Good day,) "Dag" (Goodbye) and "Dank" (Thank you.)

● This fall, plant tulip bulbs for your students to enjoy in the spring, or bring in several types of Dutch cheese for them to sample and enjoy. (Edam, Gouda and Muenster.)

● Read the story or show the film "Hans Brinker and the Silver Skates" to your class.

The
Netherlands

The Flag of The Netherlands

Greece

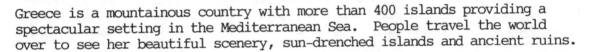

Capital City: Athens

Main Language: Greek

Currency: Drachma

Area: 50,942 sq. mi. (131,940 sq. km.)

Population: 9,988,000

Main Religions: Christian, Islam

Government: Republic

People: Greek

Flag: The design of the Greek flag was inspired by the "Stars and Stripes" of America. The Greeks incorporated the cross, the symbol of Christianity.

Greece is a mountainous country with more than 400 islands providing a spectacular setting in the Mediterranean Sea. People travel the world over to see her beautiful scenery, sun-drenched islands and ancient ruins.

Most of the Greek people live in rural areas or fishing villages. Many tend goats and sheep, spinning and weaving the wool into colorful costumes. Fishermen gather sponges and fish for many sea foods from the Mediterranean.

Ancient Greece was the birthplace of democracy. Early scholars such as Plato, Hippocrates and Socrates gave the western world many important ideas. Aristotle argued that the earth was round, 1800 years before Columbus made his first voyage.

The ancient Greeks believed in many gods and Mount Olympus was thought to be the home of Zeus, the most powerful god. About 150 miles south of Olympus lies the capital city of Athens. It was here, in 490 B.C., a runner raced from the battlefield of Marathon to Anthens with the news of the defeat of the Persian army. His run of 26 miles (42 km) inspired the first Olympic games.

Greece won her independence from Turkey in 1830. A group of soldiers overtook the monarchy government of Greece in 1967. In 1975, Greece became the republic it is today.

Interesting Facts:

- The Greek Parthenon is a temple constructed of marble and is adorned with gold. It was built 200 feet above the city of Athens and contained statues of all the Greek gods. It was completed in 432 B.C.

- The first recorded ancient Olympic Games were held in Olympia, Greece, in 776 B.C.

- The first modern Olympic Games were held in Athens in 1896.

- Mount Olympus, the highest peak in Greece, was known to the ancient Greeks as "home of the gods."

- Greek was the first European language to have a written form. The word "alphabet" comes from the two Greek letters "alpha" and "beta."

- At Greek weddings, it is customary to pin paper money to the clothes of the bride and groom.

Important Holidays:

- Easter is a special holiday in Greece. The first course of the Easter meal begins with eggs that have been dyed red. Next, comes a special soup called "mayiritsa," which is made of the internal organs of the Easter lamb. A salad is served topped with sardines followed by roast lamb and rice dressing. After the huge meal, family members visit friends and neighbors. Usually a festive dance follows.

- Greek National Day is October 28th.

- On January 8th, Midwife's Day or Women's Day is celebrated in honor of all women and midwives. On this day, women stop doing housework and spend their time in leisure while men do all the household chores and look after the children.

Famous People:

- Hippocrates, the first Greek physician, is known as the "Father of Medicine."

- Alexander the Great, King of Macedonia, conquered the area of Greece. Throughout his empire he spread Greek architecture, sculpture and science.

- Pericles, architect of the Parthenon, a marble temple honoring the goddess Athena, was born about 490 B.C.

Some Things To Do:

- Write the Greek alphabet on the chalkboard.

- Conduct your own classroom Olympics by holding a marathon spelling bee, math quiz sprint or library book decathalon. Award gold, silver and bronze medals.

- Teach your students the Greek phrases; "Yaisou" (Hello,) "Andio" (Good bye) and "Bfeharisto" (Thank you.)

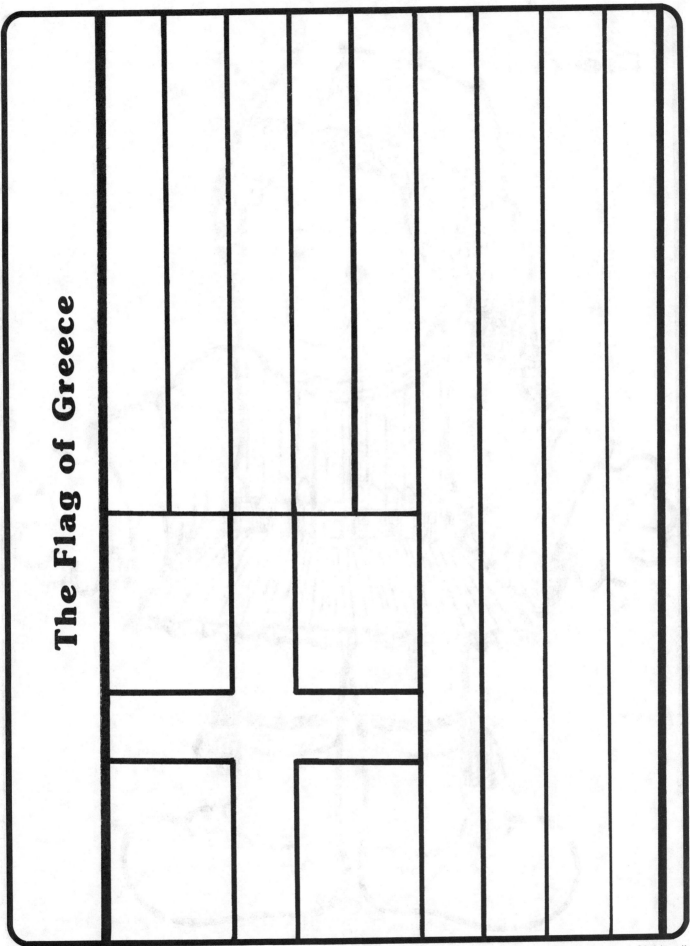

The Flag of Greece

Greece

Greece

Israel

Capital City: Tel Aviv, Jerusalem

Main Languages: Hebrew, Arabic, Yiddish

Currency: Israeli Pound - New Shekel

Area: 8,019 sq. mi. (20,770 sq. km.)

Population: 4,223,000

Main Religions: Jewish and Moslem

Government: Republic

People: Israelis

Flag: The Israeli flag consists of the six-pointed Star of David, the national Jewish emblem.

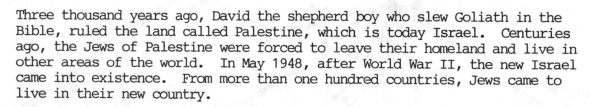

Three thousand years ago, David the shepherd boy who slew Goliath in the Bible, ruled the land called Palestine, which is today Israel. Centuries ago, the Jews of Palestine were forced to leave their homeland and live in other areas of the world. In May 1948, after World War II, the new Israel came into existence. From more than one hundred countries, Jews came to live in their new country.

The land of Israel has been called the "land of milk and honey." But, farming has been difficult in the mostly dry and desert plains. Many Jews established "kibbutzim," cooperative farms, where members share in the chores and the harvest. With modern science, Israelis have formed successful irrigation systems and replenished the soil to provide profitable crops. Mining and manufacturing are also valuable industries. Most Israelis live and work in the modern towns and cities.

Tel Aviv is considered the international capital of Israel, but most Jews observe Jerusalem as their capital city. Jerusalem is a holy city to all Jews, Christians and Moslems. No other city in the world is so important to such a great number of people with such different beliefs. Several shrines, ruins and monuments attract thousands of visitors each year to "The Holy Land."

The ten High Holy Days of Rosh Hashanah and Yom Kippur offer the Jews a time to remember the past and to express hope for the future. These days are very sacred to the Jewish people. It is a special time for people to attend services in temples and synagogues. At these services and family gatherings, Jews ask for God's forgiveness and vow to better themselves and their actions toward others in the future.

From the time the new nation was formed, Israel has fought with its Arab neighbors over boundary differences. There have been several short wars which left Israel with control of land which belonged to Syria, Jordon and Egypt. Today, the fighting still goes on even though negotiations continue. Peace seems to come slowly to the area even though the Hebrew greeting "shalom" means "peace."

Interesting Facts:

- The land around the Dead Sea is the lowest recorded point on earth at 1,296 feet (or 1½ miles) below sea level.

- Jerusalem is the second oldest city in the world, about 3000 B.C. (Only Gaziantep, Turkey, is older, 3650 B.C.)

- Israel is the only nation where children teach their parents their mother tongue, Hebrew. Hebrew had not been widely used for almost 2,000 years. Today Hebrew is taught in the schools.

- The name Jerusalem means "foundation of peace."

Important Holidays:

- Passover, today, is observed usually during the month of April and is celebrated by Jewish families by eating a ceremonial dinner and retelling the story of the exodus of the Jews from Egypt.

- Rosh Hashanah, in September, marks the Jewish New Year, the beginning of the High Holy Days. The story of Abraham is read and families celebrate by eating round loaves of bread and apples dipped in honey.

- Yom Kippur or "Day of Atonement" is the holiest day in the Jewish calendar. On this day in September or October, Jews ask forgiveness of their sins and pray to God that they will live well in the New Year.

- Jewish families celebrate Hanukkah, (in December) in memory of the defeat of the Syrians by the Maccabees. This "Feast of Lights" is commemorated with the lighting of one candle each night of the eight day festival. Songs, stories and presents are shared by everyone in the family.

Famous People:

- Moses, the great leader and lawgiver of the Jews, led them out of Egypt.

- David, the second King of Israel. He organized the Jewish tribes into a national state, about 950 B.C.

- David Ben-Gurion was the first prime minister of new Israel. He was born in 1886.

- Golda Meir, first woman prime minister of Israel, born in 1898.

Some Things To Do:

- Serve your students "latkes" potato pancakes with applesauce in celebration of Hanukkah.

- Teach your students these Hebrew phrases: "Shalom" (Hello and Goodbye) and "Todah" (Thank you.)

- Have students cut three exact triangles from construction paper and make a Star of David.

Israel

Israel

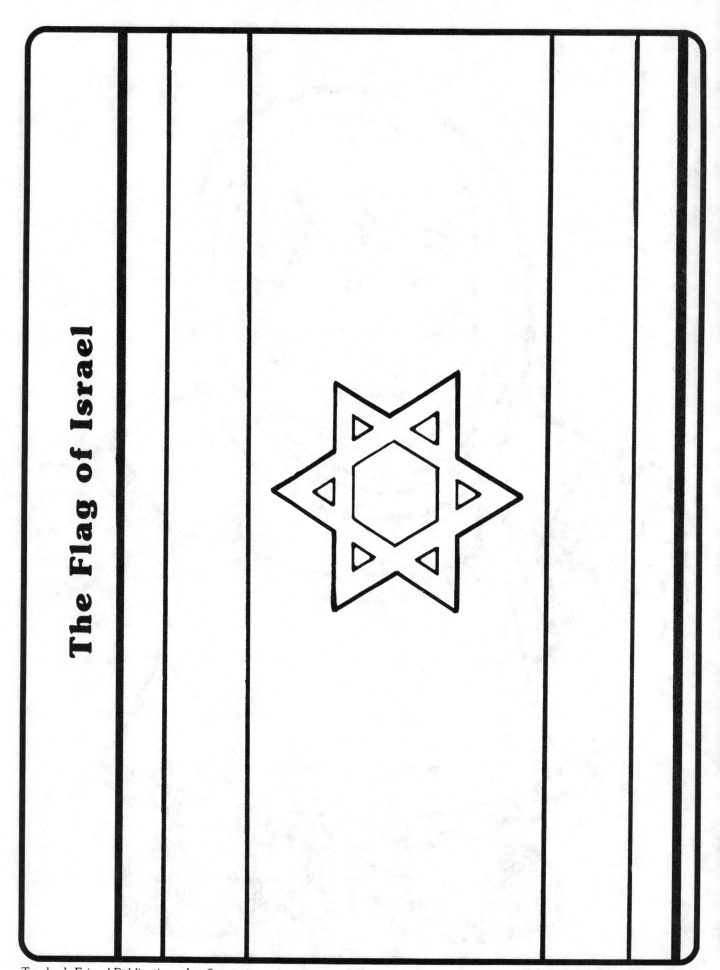

The Flag of Israel

Saudi Arabia

Capital City: Riyadh

Main Language: Arabic

Currency: Saudi Riyal

Area: 829,996 sq. mi. (2,149,690 sq. km.)

Population: 14,905,000

Main Religion: Moslem (Islam)

Government: Monarchy

People: Saudis or Saudi Arabians

Flag: The Arabic words on the flag state, "There is no god but God and Muhammad is his Prophet."

Saudi Arabia is a large country in the Middle East and the birthplace of the religion of Islam. Five times a day, Moslems around the world pray and bow toward the holy city of Mecca. Thousands of Moslems each year travel to Mecca to worship in the Great Mosque. They believe in one God, Allah and in his special prophet Muhammad. Muhammad was born in Mecca over 1,400 years ago. He wrote the Koran, a holy book that Moslems use as the supreme law of the land.

Most of the land in Saudi Arabia is desert. It is normal for temperatures to exceed 120 degrees fahrenheit. In the Rub al Khali, or "Great Sandy Desert," rain has not fallen in years. Here, Bedouin tribesmen roam the desert herding camels, goats and sheep. They live in tents with the women separated from the men.

Farming is difficult in this hot, dry nation. Even grass to feed animals is scarce. Towns and villages have sprung up from fertile oases where the only crops are grown.

The country of Saudi Arabia was created after World War I by the Saudi tribe of the Wahhabis. They led the way in uniting a large section of the Middle East pennisula. The Saudi Royal Family is the ruling force, supported by the strict religious laws.

Saudi Arabia has one main resource and that is oil. Large oil tankers can be seen in the Persian Gulf on their way to deliver oil to Europe and North America. Oil has given the nation tremendous wealth and world power.

Even with the Saudis' new found wealth, they value their Bedouin past and follow the Koran as their guide. Smoking, liquor and music is prohibited throughout the country. Outside the home, women must wear a veil to cover their faces at all times. Attendance at mosques is always required.

Interesting Facts:

- The Persian Gulf is the warmest of all seas with a temperature of about 80 degrees fahrenheit.

- At least once in their lifetime, each Moslem is to visit the holy city of Mecca and pray at the holy building, "Kaaba."

- Arabic is the second most widely used alphabet in the world. The Arabic language is written from right to left.

- When in the presence of a Bedouin nomad, it is rude to show the soles of your feet or touch your food with your left hand.

- Arab women must cover themselves from head to foot before going out-side their homes. Many times they must wear long black robes and veils or masks across their faces.

Important Holidays:

- At the end of April, Lailat al-Miraj marks a special night in the life of the prophet Muhammad. It is told that on this night, Allah pre-scribed that all Moslems pray five times a day.

- Ramadan, celebrated in the ninth month of the Islamic calendar, is devoted to fasting. Everyone, except children and the very old, may not eat or drink from sunrise to sunset.

- Awwal Muharram, in September, marks the flight of the prophet Mu-hammad and his escape to Medina where he was able to worship Allah freely. This day marks the first day of the Islamic calendar or New Year's Day.

Important People:

- Islam was founded by Muhammad, the prophet, in Medina, Saudi Arabia in 622 A.D.

Some Things To Do:

- In the markets of Saudi Arabia very little money is exchanged. In-stead, people barter or trade for goods. Have your students bring in items from home to barter with other students.

- Teach your students this Arabic phrase; "Mar-huba, iss-mee _____." (Hello, my name is _____.)

- Have your students write a short poem from right to left in order to better understand how the Arabic language is written.

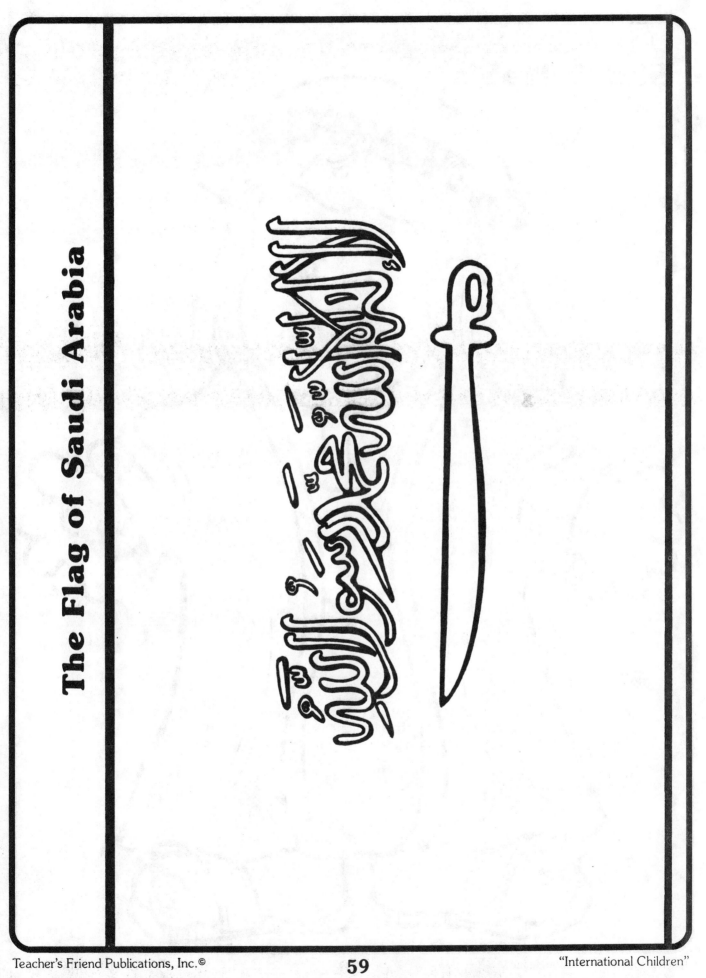

The Flag of Saudi Arabia

Saudi Arabia

Saudi Arabia

Russia

Capital City: Moscow

Main Language: Russian

Currency: Ruble

Area: 6,592,800 sq. mi. (17,075,400 sq. km.)

Population: 185 million

Main Religions: Christian, Moslem and Jewish

Government: (newly formed) Republic

People: Russian

Flag: The new Russian flag is represented with three horizontal stripes. The top stripe is white and stands for nobility. The middle blue stripe stands for fidelity and the bottom red stripe for courage.

The United Soviet Socialist Republics had been the largest country in the world. It was made up of fifteen separate republics, the largest being Russia.

Russia grew up around the area of Moscow in the fifteenth century. Under such absolute rulers as Catherine the Great, Peter the Great and Ivan the Terrible, Russia expanded her boundaries to enormous proportions. Siberia was added during the 1600's.

In 1917, the Russian Revolution took place and communist rule was declared. Under Nikolai Lenin in 1922, the country was proclaimed "The Union of Soviet Socialist Republics." Over the next few decades and the second world war, many neighboring countries were conquered and added to the huge nation.

Today, the U.S.S.R. does not exist as we once knew it. In only three days in 1991, the Soviet people demanded the overthrow of the communist government and the independence of each republic. The world rejoiced in the new freedom obtained by the Soviet and Russian people.

Because of its size, Russia has vast resources. Oil, gas, coal and gold have been found in Siberia. But, the economy of Russia, with the overthrow of the Communist Party, is in a poor way. Russian industries have not been competitive in the world market and adequate food and services have diminished. It is not uncommon for people to wait hours in line to buy bread or other essentials.

Moscow, the capital city, has been the center for all transportation, industry and education as well as the seat of government. The Kremlin stands in the heart of the city. Within the walls of the Kremlin rise beautiful churches, palaces and bell towers. Outside the walls is Red Square. On the other side is the Cathedral of St. Basil with its nine magnificent onion-shaped domes. All roads lead out from the center of Moscow.

Russia, today, is struggling to form a new democratic government, free from oppression. The Russian people have much hope for a happier and more prosperous tomorrow.

Interesting Facts:

- The name "Russia" comes from the word "Rus" used by the Slavic people for whom others called "Vikings."

- The deepest lake in the world is Lake Baykal at 6,365 feet deep, or 4,872 feet below sea level.

- The Caspian Sea is the largest lake in the world. It is 152,085 square miles.

- The Russian famine of 1914-1924 was the worst of all time. It left 20 million people dead.

- Over seventy-five percent of the Russian women work side by side with men in daily jobs. Women comprise 50% of the country's doctors, educators and economists.

Important Holidays:

- Women's Day, March 8th, is observed as a national holiday. Women workers are presented with gifts and flowers by their male counterparts.

- August 12th is National Sports Day. This annual holiday is regarded as a festival of health, beauty and fitness.

- The Mushroom Harvest is held on the 12th of September. On this day, Belorussian families get up early to pick as many mushrooms as possible. The first thing a gatherer learns is how to identify poisonous mushrooms from good ones.

Famous People:

- The Russian composer, Peter Tchaikovsky, composed the music for "The Nutcracker" ballet.

- Leo Tolstoy, Russian author of War and Peace was born in 1829.

- Alexander Solzhenitsyn, Soviet novelist and winner of the 1970 Nobel Prize for Literature, was born in 1918.

Some Things To Do:

- In Russian Cossack dancing, men do high kicks and wild somersaults. Perhaps your students would like to try Cossack dancing.

- The military parades of May Day are probably in the past, but May 1st might be a wonderful day to celebrate the newly achieved freedom of the Russian people.

- Russian is written in the Cyrillic alphabet. You may like to teach your students this Russian phrase; "Is-drast-vooey-ti-ey men-yah zov-wot _____," (Hello, my name is _____.)

Russia

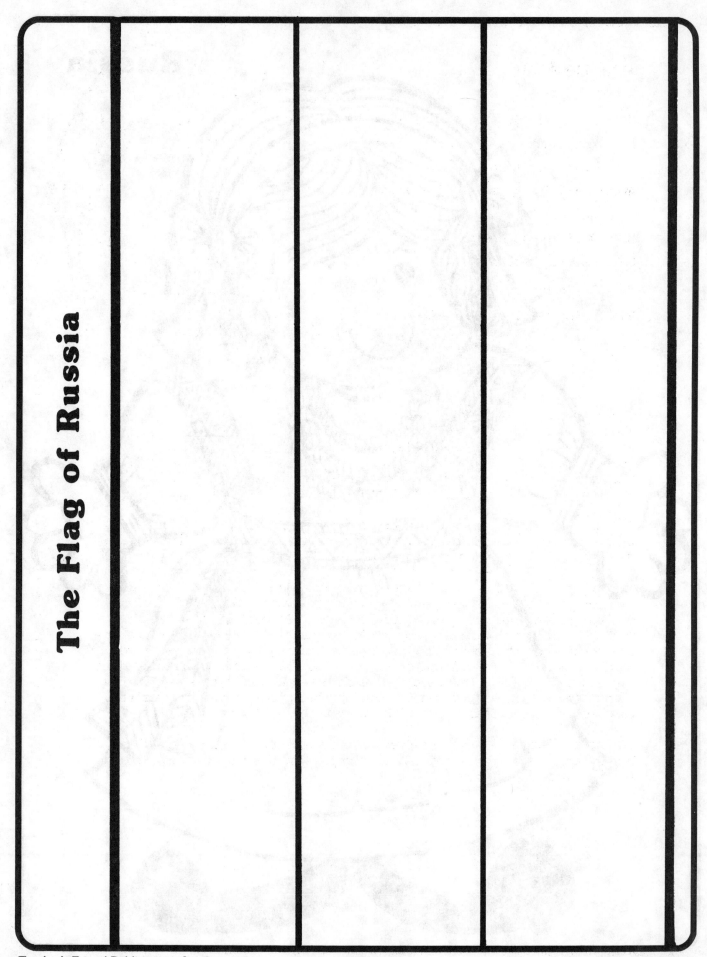

The Flag of Russia

Tunisia

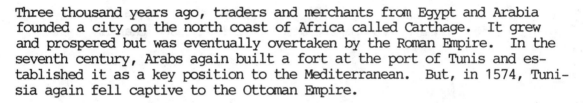

Capital City: Tunis

Main Languages: Arabic and French

Currency: Tunisian Dinar

Area: 63,170 sq. mi. (163,610 sq. km.)

Population: 7,565,000

Main Religions: Moslem, Jewish, Christian

Government: Republic

People: Tunisian

Flag: The red crescent and star signify a Moslem state. The white circle stands for unity and the red background for the blood shed. These are all modern meanings given to a very old flag.

Three thousand years ago, traders and merchants from Egypt and Arabia founded a city on the north coast of Africa called Carthage. It grew and prospered but was eventually overtaken by the Roman Empire. In the seventh century, Arabs again built a fort at the port of Tunis and established it as a key position to the Mediterranean. But, in 1574, Tunisia again fell captive to the Ottoman Empire.

In 1881, France seized the country and remained in control until independence was achieved in 1956. It was the following year that Tunisia declared itself a republic and began self rule.

The dry sands of the Sahara Desert give Tunisian villagers little protection from the harsh elements. Here, few crops grow and the people dig homes into the walls of cliffs to seek cool comfort in the earth. The Sahara Desert comprises about 40% of Tunisia's land. In the southern portion of the country it is very hot during the day and extremely cold at night. A record temperature of 130° fahrenheit was recorded in the Sahara in 1922. Few people live here because of little water, few plants and no animals to hunt. Nomad tribes often travel the desert by camel caravan to trade goods with other tribes and settlements.

The northeastern valleys, however, receive plenty of rain where wheat, barley and olive groves dot the landscape. In these lush areas, towns and villages flourish.

Interesting Facts:

● Most Tunisians daily eat a coarse porridge made of wheat flour called "cous-cous." They eat it with vegetables and a spicy sauce.

● During the 400 years of the Roman conquest, the Romans built over 180 cities in Tunisia.

● On the central coast of Tunisia is the "Forest of Olive Trees." The 1½ million acres contain over eight million trees. Tunisia is the world's second largest exporter of olive oil.

● Tunisia is one of the few Moslem countries where women can divorce their husbands.

Important Holidays:

● March 20th marks the holiday commemorating Tunisian independence.

● The Tree Festival of Tunisia is held every second Sunday in November. The day is celebrated with a large agricultural fair.

● Women's Day, August 13th is held in honor of all Tunisian women. (Tunisian women have more freedom and independence than any other Moslem country.)

Famous People:

● Habib Bourguiba, first president of Tunisia, has given the women of his country enhanced independence.

Some Things To Do:

● The main language of Tunisia is Arabic. Write the Arabic alphabet on the class board.

● Introduce your students to some native crops of Tunisia, such as; olives and dates.

● The village people and Nomad tribesmen often trade goods rather than using currency. Arrange a day for your students to bring items from home and trade them with other students.

The Arabic Alphabet

خ د ذ ر ز س ش ص ض ط ظ
ع غ ف ق ك ل ش ص ض ط ظ
م ن هـ و ي

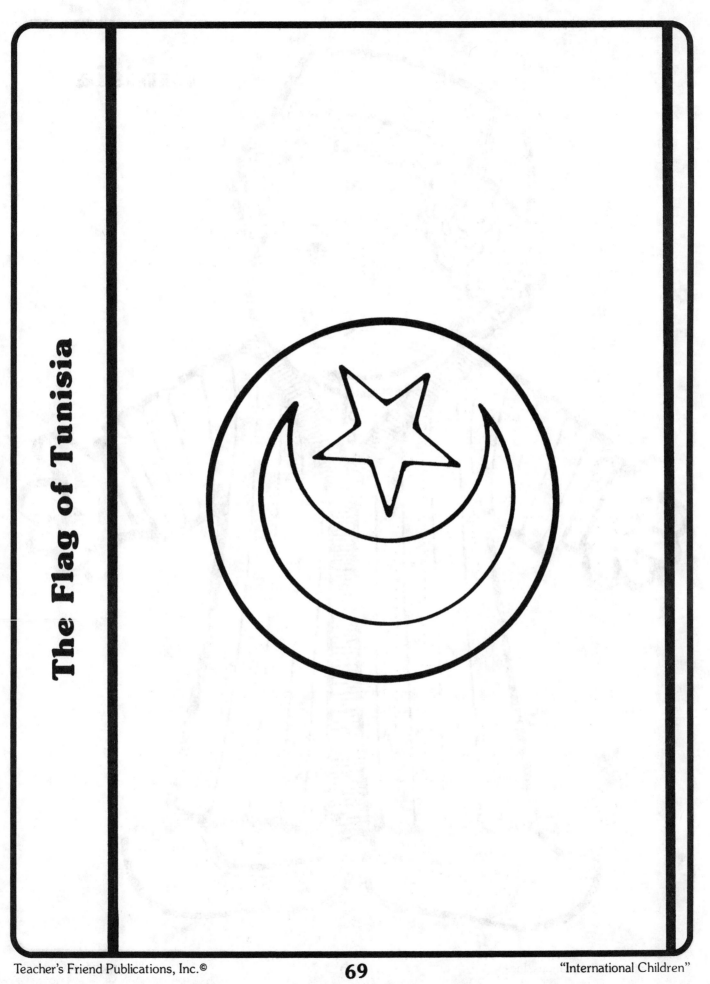

The Flag of Tunisia

Tunisia

Kenya

Capital City: Nairobi

Main Languages: Swahili, English and tribal languages

Currency: Kenyan Shilling

Area: 224,081 sq. mi. (580,367 sq. km.)

Population: 23,000,000

Main Religions: Christian and tribal religions

Government: Republic

People: Kenyans

Flag: The black stripe on the Kenyan flag stands for the majority of the people, the red for independence and the green for agriculture. The thin white stripes represent the non-African minorities. A traditional African shield is pictured in the center.

The people of Kenya consist of many different African tribes as well as Arabs, Europeans and Indians. The Kikuyus are the largest tribe of Kenya. Legend has it that a great tribal god, Ngai (Divider of the Universe,) created the sacred Mount Kenya and gave its fertile highlands to the Kikuyus. Kenya was named for Mount Kenya. Today, most of the people live in this prosperous region or near the shores of Lake Victoria or the Indian Ocean.

In 1887, Europeans first came to the area of Kenya. At that time, the land was ruled by the Sulton of Zanzibar. Great Britain established communities in Zanzibar and on the coasts of Kenya. Their claimed area also included Uganda.

Kenya was the stage for several wars of liberation including the Mau Mau Rebellion. In 1963, Kenya became independent and Jomo Kenyatta was declared the first prime minister. With his leadership, Kenya proved to be one of the strongest African nations.

Farming and ranching are Kenya's main occupations. It is not unusual for a young warrior to defend his family's cattle from the attack of a lion. The dry plains of southwest Kenya is home to many wild animals. Much of the wildlife is protected in several large national parks.

Many of the people of the plains region still live in small villages with mud huts and no modern conveniences. However, the capital city of Nairobi is a modern metropolis with tall buildings and up-to-date services.

Interesting Facts:

● Lake Victoria is the third largest lake in the world at 26,828 sq. mi.

● There are more than 1,000 different languages in Africa. Many are only spoken languages and have no written form.

● One half of the population of Kenya is less than 16 years old.

● Among the Kikuyu tribe, the more ornaments a man wears on his ears, the more his fellow villagers will respect him.

● The equator runs right through the middle of Kenya.

Important Holidays:

● December 12th is Kenya's Independence Day or "Jamhuri Day." This festive day commemorates the proclamation making Kenya a republic in 1963.

● The largest agricultural and technological fair in Africa is held in October in the capital city of Nairobi. It is an honor for farmers to be chosen to display prize potatoes, carrots and cattle.

● June 1st is "Madaraka Day" or Self-Rule Day. It is observed as a national holiday.

Famous People:

● In 1963, President Jomo Kenyatta led the country to independence from British rule. His slogan was "Harambee," swahili for "Let all pull together."

● Daniel arap Moi became the second president of Kenya in 1978.

Some Things To Do:

● Teach your students these Swahili phrases; "Jambo" (Hello,) "Kwaheri" (Goodbye) and "Asante" (Thank you.)

● Introduce your students to several tropical fruits such as papaya, pineapple and guava.

● As an art project, have students make their own African shields and decorate them in various ways.

Kenya

Kenya

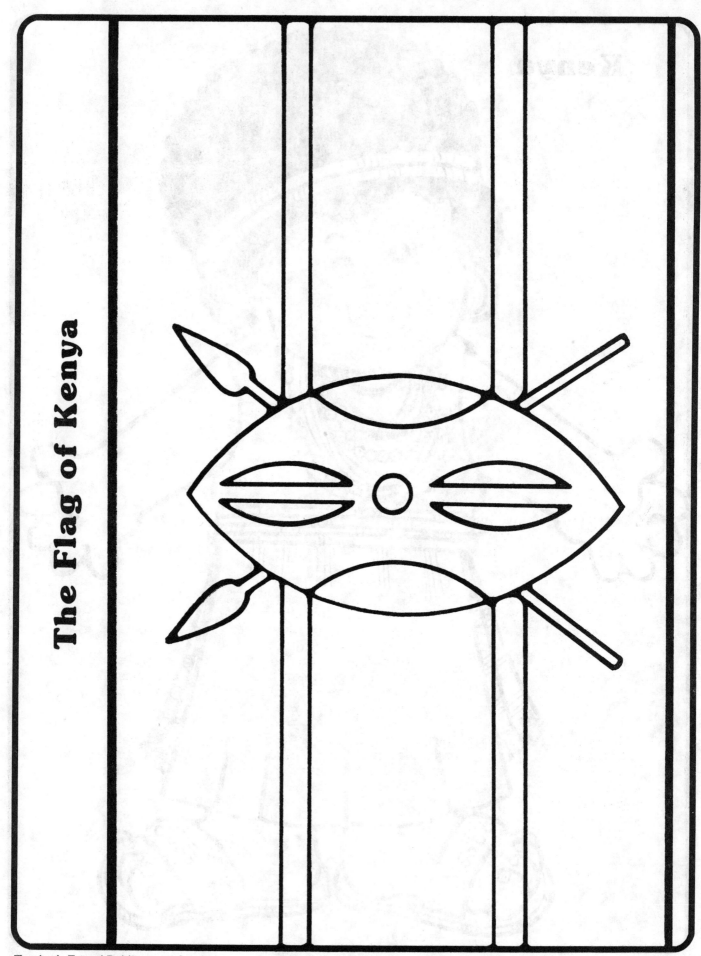

The Flag of Kenya

India

Capital City: New Delhi

Main Languages: Hindi and English

Currency: Rupee

Area: 1,269,340 sq. mi. (3,287,590 sq. km.)

Population: 800,330,000

Main Religions: Hindu, Moslem, Christian, Sikh, Buddhist

Government: Republic

People: Indians

Flag: India's flag represents the people of various religions united into one country. The orange stripe stands for Hindu, the green for Moslem, the white for peace and the wheel of Ashoka for Buddhists.

Over 800 million people live in India. Most live in villages and farm the land. It is difficult to grow the large amounts of food needed by the huge population. No matter how hard the families work, there is seldom enough food to go around.

Weather is a tremendous problem in India. Most of the rain falls in one season, called the monsoon, (June through September.) The rest of the year, it is hot and dry until the rains of the monsoon begin again.

An ancient set of rules, called the caste system, is still observed in much of India today. These rules restrict people from socializing or mixing with any other group of people except those of their ancestors. But, this old way of thinking is slowly breaking down.

Four out of five Indians are Hindus. In the Hindu religion, cattle are regarded as sacred and it is forbidden to eat beef. It is not unusual to see great numbers of cattle free to eat valuable food crops while roaming the countryside. They can also be seen on the city streets.

India's traditions are deeply rooted in religion and greatly influence their music, customs, costumes, dance and festivals. The people love to dress in colorful fabrics of silks and cottons. Women wear beautiful "saris," dresses made of a length of material (5-9 meters long) and wrapped around their bodies. The borders of the saris are often trimmed with silver or gold thread.

Interesting Facts:

- The Taj Mahal, built in 1654, is an exquisite tomb built in honor of a queen. It is made of brilliant white marble and colorful jewels cover the doors and windows.

- Indian women often wear rings in their nose to show that they are married.

- Numerals were invented in India in about 300 B.C.

- The one hundred rupee note contains the same words written in eight different Indian languages plus English.

- India's four castes consists of: "Brahmans" (Priests,) "Kshatriyas" (Nobles and Warriors,) "Vaisyas" (Traders) and "Sudras" (Serfs.) There are also millions of people considered "Untouchables" that live in enforced poverty, below the caste system.

Important Holidays:

- On October 2nd, the Indian people observe the birthday of Mohandas Gandhi, the "Father of India." On this day quiet time is spent spinning cotton thread and singing devotional songs in his memory.

- The Pushkar Fair is held in celebration of Brahma the Creator. The Hindu people worship in Brahma's temple and spend four days buying, selling and trading different animals, especially camels.

- India's national holiday, Republic Day, is celebrated on January 26th. It is joyously celebrated for two days.

- In different areas of India, the Hindu New Year is marked by the Diwali festival. Families decorate doorways with intricate designs of rice flour to welcome the goddess of wealth. It is also known as the Festival of Lights with fireworks and bonfires playing an important role in the festivities.

Famous People:

- Mohandas Gandhi, known as the "Father of India" was born in 1869.

- Buddhism was founded by Prince Siddhartha Gautama (the Buddah) in India in about 500 B.C.

- Jawaharlal Nehru, first prime minister of India, was born in 1889.

- Indira Gandhi, woman prime minister of India, (1966-77 and 1980-84.)

Some Things To Do:

- Burn an incense candle in celebration of the Diwali festival.

- A special meal in India might include rice, lentils and curried vegetables. Introduce the flavor of curry to your students.

- Bring a length of fabric to class and have students take turns wrapping saris.

The Flag of India

India

81

China

Capital City: Peking (Beijing)

Main Language: Mandarin Chinese

Currency: Yuan

Area: 3,705,390 sq. mi. (9,596,961 sq. km.)

Population: 1,051,000,000

Main Religion: Buddhist

Government: Communist Republic

People: Chinese

Flag: The large star stands for communism and the four small stars represent the four classes of society.

China has more people than any other country with a population of over one billion people!

Most of the Chinese people work at farming because a great deal of food is needed to feed the population. Rice and wheat are China's main crops.

In 1949, the Communists, led by Mao Tse-tung, took control of all China except for the island of Taiwan. The new government took control of all the land and industries. In recent years, trade has been established with other countries. If you look around your own home, you are sure to find something manufactured in China.

The Chinese language has many dialects. The most widely used is Mandarin Chinese. The ancient Chinese language was written using thousands of symbols and characters. It was also written from top to bottom. Today, a new form of the Chinese language has been developed using the Roman alphabet and is written from left to right.

The Chinese New Year is perhaps the most colorful and joyous celebration of the year. It marks the beginning of a new cycle of life and symbolizes the end of winter and the beginning of spring. It is celebrated the first three weeks with the beginning of the new moon of the lunar calendar. (It may fall anywhere between the middle of January to the beginning of March.)

On the third day of the New Year, the Chinese people celebrate the "Feast of the Lanterns!" Lanterns of all shapes, colors and sizes decorate the streets and houses. Many cities hold fantastic parades led by a huge dragon, the symbol of good luck.

Interesting Facts:

- One out of five people in the world is Chinese.

- The Great Wall of China is 3,900 miles long. It took at least one million people working twenty-five years to complete.

- Ketchup (or ke-tsiap) originated in China and was a sauce of fish broth and mushrooms. The English added tomatoes and it became "ketchup!"

- The second most populous city in the world is Shanghai, with thirteen million people.

  The Chinese were the first to use paper money, in the 8th century A.D.

- Gunpowder was first invented in China to make beautiful fireworks.

Important Holidays:

- Vesak, in May, is the most important festival of the Buddhist year. It commemorates the birth, enlightenment and death of the founder of Buddhism. On this day, villagers construct rockets decorated with flowers and streamers. A contest is held to see which will go the farthest.

- The Dragon Boat Festival takes place on June 18th. On this day, colorful boat races are held in honor of a great statesman, Ch'u Yuan. Each boat has the head of a dragon on its prow and can seat as many as fifty rowers.

Famous People:

- Confucius, the Chinese philosopher was born in 551 B.C.
- Sun Yat-sen, founder of the Republic of China.
- Genghis Khan, powerful leader of the Mongolian Empire.
- Prince Siddhartha Gautama (the Buddha,) founder of Buddhism.

Some Things To Do:

- Make paper lanterns to decorate the classroom.
- Teach your students to use chopsticks.
- Write the words "Huan Ying" (Welcome) on the class chalkboard.
- Prepare rice and stir-fried vegetables in the classroom.
- Ask your students to find out the names of the animals of the Chinese Zodiac.
- Bring fortune cookies to school to share with your students.
- Ask students to write their own creative fortunes.

China

China

Flag of the People's Republic of China

Japan

Capital City: Tokyo

Main Language: Japanese

Currency: Yen

Area: 143,749 sq. mi. (372,310 sq. km.)

Population: 122,125,000

Main Religions: Buddhist and Shinto

Government: Constitutional Monarchy

People: Japanese

Flag: The white background of the Japanese flag is said to stand for purity and integrity and the red "rising sun" for sincerity, brightness and warmth.

Japan consists of four large islands and hundreds of small ones off the coast of Asia. The islands are very mountainous and must be terraced to provide enough farmland to feed the large population. The fishing industry helps to provide seafood and seaweed harvesting, but some food must be imported from other countries.

In spite of Japan's lack of resources, it has grown to be one of the most wealthy nations on earth. The people of Japan have developed successful industries with advanced technologies. Most of the manufactured goods are sold to other countries. This is how Japan has acquired its wealth.

Japan has a long history. The first Japanese Emperor began his rule in 660 B.C. Many armies attempted to conquer Japan, but all failed. In the 16th century, Europeans came to the area to trade goods. The Japanese were distrustful of the foreigners and isolated themselves from the outside world until 1853. It was Commodore Perry of the United States Navy that persuaded the Emperor to open Japan to western trade and ideas. Quickly, the Japanese moved into the modern age.

Tokyo is the capital city of Japan and the largest in the world with over 24 million people. The city's western life-style and hard-working habits represent the spirit of the new Japan. Tokyo is a colorful city with neon-lit streets at night. The city is crowded with shoppers looking for bargains and diners enjoying "sushi," (raw fish and rice.) Because it is so crowded, traveling in Tokyo is difficult. Some streets are not even named which makes it nearly impossible to find one's way around. The city dwellers home reflects the old and the new. It is not unusual to find modern televisions and appliances next to charcoal burning stoves and ancient utensils.

Japan's people are both courteous and formal. It is customary that they greet each other by bowing. Their spectacular temples and beautiful gardens and colorful ceremonies reflect the gentle qualities of these hard-working people.

Interesting Facts:

- The word Japan means "land of the rising sun."

- The most expensive city in the world to live is Tokyo, Japan.

- Mt. Fujiyama, in Japan, is painted and photographed more than any other mountain in the world.

- The official legend of Imperial Japan claims that the descendant of the Sun Goddess, Jimmu Tenno, established the nation in 660 B.C. His descendants continue to rule Japan today.

- The Japanese alphabet has more than 1,800 different characters.

Important Holidays:

- Children's Day is celebrated on May 5th. Fish kites are flown as a showing of strength, courage and determination. These are the qualities elders wish for the children of Japan.

- The Sapporo Snow Festival is celebrated on February 6th. It is a popular day in which contests are held for artists building the most elaborate "snowmen" or snow sculptures.

- Shoogatsu, Japan's New Year, takes place on January 1st. This is a time for everyone to clean their homes in order that good fortune will want to enter. Parties are held to help forget the old year and look forward to the new. At midnight, temple bells ring 108 times signifying the 108 human weaknesses described in the teachings of Buddha, thus helping everyone to begin anew.

- The Girl's Doll Festival takes place on March 3rd. This is a day for parents to express pride and love for their daughters. Mothers present elaborate dolls, representing the Japanese Imperial Court, to their daughters. The girls then arrange these dolls on special shelves for display. A special party usually follows.

Famous People:

- Kublai Khan, 13th century Emperor of Japan.

- Jimmu Tenno established the Japanese nation in 660 B.C.

- Buddhism was founded by Prince Siddhartha Gautama (the Buddha,) in about 500 B.C.

- Emperor Hirohito, ruler of Japan, was born in 1901.

Some Things To Do:

- Teach your students these Japanese phrases: "Ohio" (Hello,) "Sayonara" (Goodbye) and "Kansha sura" (Thank you.)

- Bring in "sushi" for your students to sample.

- Have your students write a "haiku" poem or do "origami," Japanese paper folding.

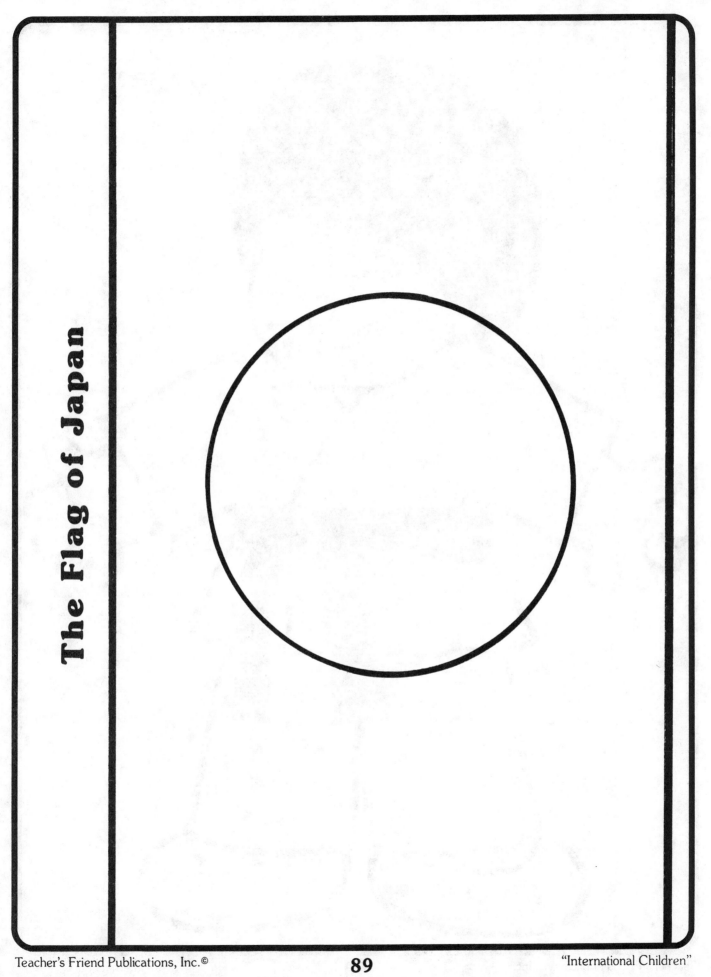

The Flag of Japan

Japan

Pacific Islands

Islands:

Easter Island – This island is under Chilean control and is famous for it's "Moai" statues.

Figi – There are about 844 Figi islands in the sourthwest Pacific. It is an independent country but was once ruled by Great Britain.

Guam – All Guamanians are United States citizens but cannot vote in Presidential elections.

Hawaii – The eight Hawaiian islands make up the 50th state of the United States of America.

French Polynesia – These 130 islands are located in the south-central Pacific. Many of the islands are not inhabited.

Samoa – Most of these fifteen islands are under U.S. control.

Tahiti – This island is the capital of French Polynesia.

(This is just a partial list of the many beautiful islands in the South Pacific.)

There are thousands of islands in the Pacific Ocean. They are under the control of a variety of other nations including, Great Britain, Chile, Japan, France and the United States.

Some of the islands are volcanic while others were formed by coral. Islands are tops of underwater mountains or volcanos. Only the tallest mountains can make an island. Some islands were made by coral polyps. These small sea creatures form a rock-hard substance that over thousands of years form coral reefs and islands.

Most of the islands have few natural resources and must rely on tourism, farming and fishing to provide for their people. The warm tropical climate provides farmers with a variety of fruits and tropical crops that are shipped to other parts of the world. Pineapples, bananas and sugar cane are the most common.

The people of each group of islands have slightly different characteristics. Some of the island people have very dark skin while others have light brown skin or Asian features. Each island group has their own traditions and ceremonies.

It is believed that the Pacific Islands were first inhabited by the people of Asia. They came by boat and eventually settled island after island. Some easterly islands may have been settled by South Americans.

Interesting Facts:

● Polynesia means "many islands" and includes most of the islands in the South Pacific. (There are only 130 French Polynesian islands.)

● The wettest place in the world is Mount Waialeale on Hawaii. It has an average rainfall of about 426 inches each year.

● The largest wave ever ridden by a surfer was reported to be 50 feet high. The wave hit Minole, Hawaii, on April 3, 1868.

● The Marianas Trench, off the edge of Guam, is the lowest point on earth at 38,198 feet deep. If Mount Everest, the tallest mountain in the world, were placed in the Marianas Trench it would be short 9,170 feet from reaching the surface.

● On January 23, 1960, two divers and their diving craft the "Trieste" successfully reached the bottom of the Mariana Trench. It was believed that no fish could survive the tremendous pressure of the water at that depth, but to their surprise they found fish!

● Many of the national flags of the South Pacific Islands are designated by the "Southern Cross," a constellation visible from the Southern Hemisphere and used by sailors for navigation.

Important Holidays:

● "Magellan Day" or "Discovery Day" celebrated on March 6th, commemorates the discovery of Guam in 1521.

● "Discovery Day" in Hawaii is celebrated on September 10. This holiday honors Pacific and Polynesian explorers.

● Figi celebrates its independence from Great Britain on October 10th.

● "White Sunday," October 14th, is celebrated in Western Samoa. On this day, parents give their children new white clothes and books. After the family attends church services, parents prepare a special feast and the children are the first to be served.

Important People:

● Captain James Cook, born in 1728, discovered many of the islands of the South Pacific.

● Queen Liliuokalani was the last ruling monarch of the Hawaiian Islands, from 1891-1894.

Some Things To Do:

● Ask your students to bring in freshly picked flowers and leaves and string their own leis.

● Bring in several tropical fruits for your students to sample, such as pineapples, coconuts and sugar canes.

The Flag of Western Samoa

Pacific
Islands

Pacific Islands

Canada

Capital City: Ottawa

Main Languages: English and French

Currency: Canadian Dollar

Area: 3,852,000 sq. mi. (9,976,000 sq. km.)

Population: 26 million people

Main Religion: Christian

Government: Constitutional Monarchy

People: Canadians

Flag: The Canadian flag displays a large red maple leaf on a white background. Red and white are the official colors of Canada.

Canada is the second largest country in the world, next to Russia. This rugged country is made up of thousands of beautiful coastlines, deep blue lakes, enormous grasslands, huge forests and harsh tundras.

Canada's people are just as varied as the country they live in. East of the Rockies, you can find cowboys herding cattle on the vast prairies of Alberta. The people of Quebec speak mostly French. Montreal is the largest French-speaking city in the world, outside of Paris. The Canadians of the southeast make their living in the fishing and timber industries. In Nova Scotia, it is not unusual, during festivals, to find men dressed in kilts and playing bagpipes, much like their ancestors.

Inuits live in the arctic north where they hunt seals and walrus. The word "Inuits" is an Indian word for "real people." Inuits are also called "Eskimos," which means "eaters of raw meat." The winters are severely cold in the northern regions. The temperature often stays 20° below zero for weeks at a time. However, the Inuits are able to build homes and find food which allows them to live in this harsh climate.

In 1867, the provinces of New Brunswick, Nova Scotia and Canada joined together to form the Dominion of Canada. The declaration was signed on July 1 of that year, and the new Canadian nation was born. People gather to sing the national anthem, "O Canada," at various celebrations.

Canada is divided into two sparsely populated territories, the Yukon and the Northwest, and ten provinces. Each province has its own local government. Canada also has a central parliamentary government with a prime minister.

All in all, Canada is an exciting country full of wonderful people and a wealth of natural beauty and resourses.

Interesting Facts:

- Canada has the longest coastline of any country in the world, 56,453 miles of water's edge.

- The lowest recorded temperature in Canada was recorded on January 31, 1947. It was 62 degrees below zero, (Fahrenheit.)

- Traditionally, some Canadians celebrate the new year by taking an icy plunge in the waters of various lakes and bays on January 1st.

- The word "Canada" comes from the Iroquois Indian word "Kanata," meaning "a group of huts."

- More than 2/3 of the population lives within 100 miles of the U.S. border and 90% lives within 200 miles.

- Canada is the most sparsely settled land on earth after Antarctica.

Important Holidays:

- Canada Day, July 1st, marks the day in 1867 when the British colony of Canada was given dominion. In 1982, Canadians were given complete independence. This day is marked throughout the country with family picnics and festive parades.

- The annual Lobster Carnival takes place in Nova Scotia and celebrates the end of the fishing season. People enjoy eating as much lobster as they can and various competitions and performances are held.

- Yukon Discovery Day is celebrated on August 17. It marks the day that gold was discovered on the Klondike River in 1896.

- Victoria Day, third Monday of May, celebrates Queen Victoria's birthday.

Famous People:

- French explorer, Jacques Cartier, and English explorers Martin Froblisher and Henry Hudson, all searched the waterways of Canada in hopes of finding a northwest passage to the Orient.

- John George Lambton was the first govenor-general of all British North America.

- Sir John A. Macdonald was the first elected prime minister (1867.)

Some Things To Do:

- Construct a totem pole in the classroom by using discarded boxes.

- Ask students to find out the origin of the northern lights or the "aurora borealis."

- Find out the meanings of these Eskimo terms; parka, mukluk, kayak, igloo, umiak and Inuit.

- Find out the names of the various Indian tribes in Canada.

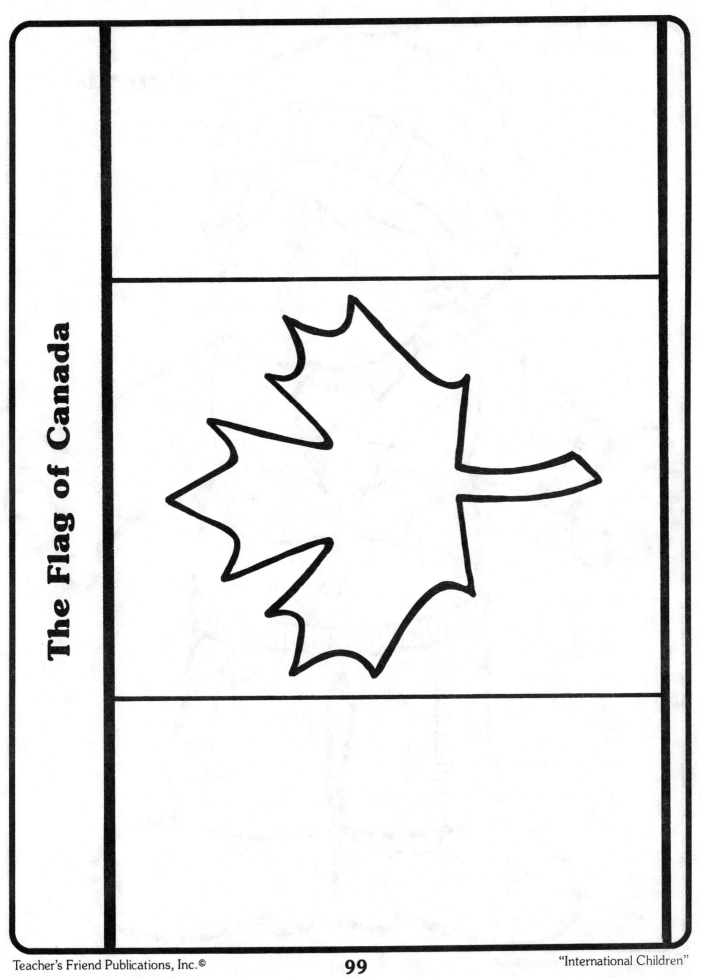

The Flag of Canada

Canada

United States of America

Capital City: Washington, D.C.

Main Languages: English and Spanish

Currency: Dollar

Area: 3,618,768 sq. mi. (9,372,610 sq. km.)

Population: 250 million

Main Religions: Christian and Jewish

Government: Democracy, Federated Union of Fifty States

People: Americans

Flag: The "Stars and Stripes" has thirteen red and white stripes representing the original thirteen colonies and 50 white stars on a blue background honoring the fifty United States.

The greatest immigration of people came soon after the Americas were discovered by Columbus. People from Spain, Holland, France, Sweden, Russia and England all claimed land in North America. Little did they know that the thirteen colonies claimed by England were to soon become the United States of America.

These first settlers built permanent settlements all along the east coast. They were a hearty bunch that had to endure great hardships. As England began to seek more control of the colonies, the colonists grew more discontented. In 1774, a small group met to organize an army to fight the English for the control of their land. George Washington was appointed commander and chief. On July 4, 1776, they adopted the Declaration of Independence, even though it took six more years of fighting before freedom from England was won. The thirteen colonies soon became the first thirteen United States.

Over time, more land was acquired by the American government by either purchase or war. Native American Indians were driven off their land in the name of American advancement. As the years followed, The United States of America stretched from the Atlantic to the Pacific Ocean, including Alaska and Hawaii as the 49th and 50th states. With this vast expanse of land and resources and the ingenuity of the American people, the U.S.A. has remained one of the most progressive and wealthiest nations in the world. It has been considered the greatest world power for decades.

People of many races make the United States their home. The country has been known as the "melting pot" of the world. The largest segment of the population is from European ancestry. Most of them came to escape famines and war. The majority of the black population has descended from slaves brought from Africa in the 18th century. Today, there is also a great population of Asians, Mexicans and Central and South Americans working for a better way of life.

Many countries of the world have tried to emmulate the freedom and democracy found in the United States. Even with the many problems facing Americans, today, they can continue to be proud of a government "of the people, by the people and for the people."

Interesting Facts:

- The U.S. has the largest government budget of any nation of the world.

- Although the U.S. only consists of about 6% of the world's population, Americans own half of the world's wealth.

- The U.S. uses more energy, has more cars, and owns more telephones and televisions than any other country.

- There were hundreds of tribes of American Indians living in North America. Today, only a few remain with most of them living on reservations.

- The highest point of North America is Mount McKinley in Alaska at 20,320 feet above sea level.

- The lowest point in North America is Death Valley, California, at 282 feet below sea level.

Important Holidays:

- Fourth of July celebrations, across the country, commemorate the independence of the United States in 1776. Families celebrate with parades, picnics, band concerts and fireworks.

- Americans celebrate Thanksgiving Day on the fourth Thursday of November, each year. On this day, families and friends attend church and gather for feasts of roast turkey with all the trimmings.

- Memorial Day, the last Monday in May, is a day in which Americans honor the soldiers who have died in wars in defense of the United States.

Famous People:

- Abraham Lincoln, the 16th president of the United States, was born in 1809. He signed the Emancipation Proclamation, which freed the slaves, in 1862.

- Thomas Alva Edison was born in 1847. His inventions number in the thousands, including the incandescent lamp, phonograph and microphone.

- Martin Luther King, Jr. was the inspired leader of the Civil Rights Movement in America. He was born in 1929.

Some Things To Do:

- Have students make collages with magazine pictures showing the various faces and traditions of the American "Melting Pot."

- Conduct your own 4th of July parade complete with bicycle floats, red, white and blue streamers and plenty of hot dogs and lemonade.

- Have students ask their parents and grandparents about their family's heritage. From which nations did they originally come?

U.S.A.

The Flag of the United States of America

Mexico

Capital City: Mexico City

Main Language: Spanish

Currency: Mexican Peso

Area: 761,602 sq. miles (1,972,550 sq. km.)

Population: 82,000,000

Main Religion: Christian

Government: Federal Republic

People: Mexicans

Flag: The eagle on the Mexican flag stands for strength and nobility, the snake for evil and dishonor and the cactus for the Mexican soil. The symbol also contains an evergreen oak and laurel branch. These signs honor and represent the heroes of Mexico.

Long before the Spaniards arrived in the New World, the tremendous civilization of the Aztec empire flourished in Mexico. Two-thousand years ago, the Aztec Indians built huge temples and pyramids. Their capital city, Tenochtitlan, was once where Mexico City stands today.

Legend states that a wise man told the Aztec leaders to search for a sign in the wilderness. The sign was to be an eagle perched on a cactus plant, holding a snake in one claw. In 1325, the sign appeared on an island in a salty lake. This is where the Aztecs built their magnificent city. The symbol of the eagle, snake and cactus can be found on the Mexican flag.

In the 1500's, Spanish treasure seekers, including Hernando Cortez, came and conquered the Indians of Mexico. In 1810, an Indian priest named Miguel Hidalgo y Costilla, spoke out against the Spanish occupation and demanded rights for the native people of Mexico. At first the revolt was successful, but Hidalgo's forces were soon defeated. It was not until 1822 when Spanish rule ended.

Much of Mexico's land is mountainous. The "Sierra Madre" enclose a high plateau where most of the people live. The rest of the country consists of dry deserts to the north and dense tropics on the southern coasts.

About one-third of the population of Mexico are farmers. A variety of fruits and vegetables are grown and shipped north to the United States. In northern Mexico, silver, gold, copper and oil are mined and drilled. The country, however, lacks sufficient farmland and industry for the fast growing population. Many families try to migrate to the United States in search of work.

The customs and traditions of the Spanish and Indian background make for a lively people. Fiestas are held on many special occasions and holidays. The streets and homes are decorated, strolling musicians play Mexican folk songs and wonderful foods are prepared in abundance. Colorful costumes and activities add to the excitement.

Interesting Facts:

- At the time of the Spanish conquest, Mexico was home to over 700 tribal groups speaking over 100 different languages.

- On special occasions, particularly Christmas, children in Mexico enjoy breaking a "piñata." A piñata is usually a clay or papier-mache container decorated in bright colors and filled with small gifts and candies. The children are blindfolded and given turns to swing at the piñata with a stick to break it. When it finally breaks, children hurry to gather up the treats.

- The pyramids of the "Sun" and "Moon," in the ancient city of Teoti-huacan, were built over 1,500 years ago.

- Mexico's domain once included all of Texas, California, Nevada, Utah, Arizona, New Mexico and parts of Colorado.

Important Holidays:

- Eight nights before Christmas, Mexicans perform the story of Joseph and Mary's search for shelter with the "Posadas Procession." After the procession, a party is held where a colorful piñata is broken and children scramble for goodies.

- "Cinco de Mayo," or May 5th, marks the victory of the battle of Puebla. Today, Mexicans everywhere celebrate with parades, dances and festivals.

- "Mexican Independence Day," September 15th, is celebrated throughout Mexico. At 11:00 pm, on the night of September 15th, everyone gives the historic yell for independence "Grito!" This yell has been a tradition since 1810 when Father Miguel Hidalgo gave the signal that launched the beginning of the revolution against the Spanish government.

Famous People:

- Father Miguel Hidalgo y Costilla stood up against the Spanish rulers by demanding freedom for the Indians of Mexico. With his stand, the Mexican Revolution began.

- Benito Juarez, great leader of the Mexican people and president from 1858-1863 and 1867 to 1872.

- Emiliano Zapata, Mexican revolutionary leader who championed land-ownership reforms from 1911 to 1916.

Some Things To Do:

- Have your class make their own piñata using several layers of paper grocery bags. Decorate with colored paper and streamers and fill with wrapped candies.

- Make "quesadillas" in the classroom using flour tortillas and cheese.

- Teach your students to count to ten in Spanish or use these phrases: "Buenos Dias" (Good Day) and "Adios amigos" (Goodbye friends.)

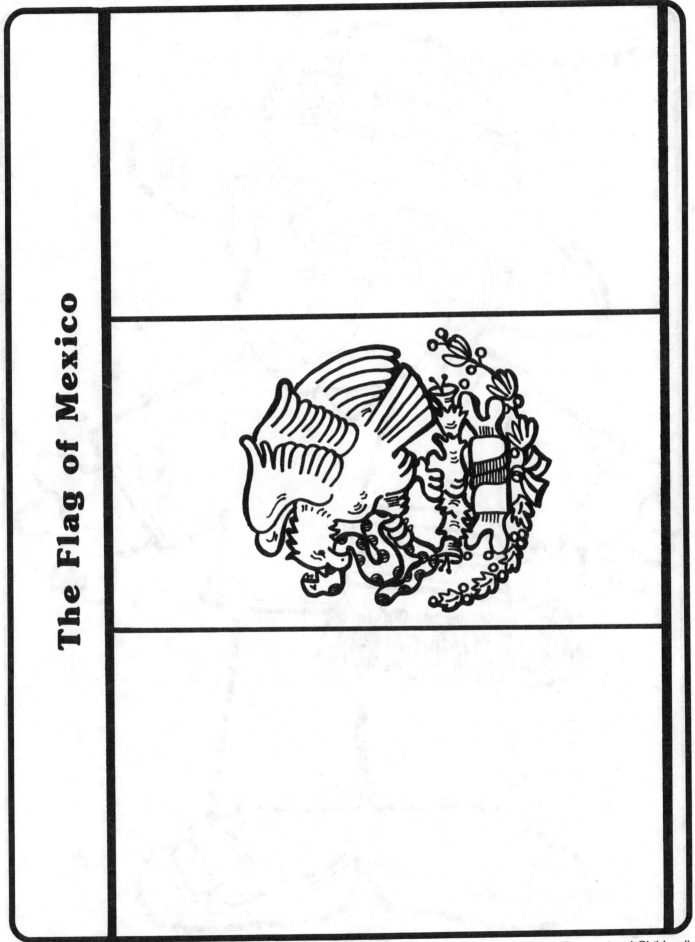

The Flag of Mexico

Mexico

Mexico

Venezuela

Capital City: Caracas

Main Language: Spanish

Currency: Bolivar

Area: 352,143 sq. mi. (912,050 sq. km.)

Population: 18,292,000

Main Religion: Christian

Government: Republic

People: Venezuelans

Flag: The flag is yellow, blue and red with seven stars in the center.

Hundreds of years ago, Spanish explorers came to the northern sections of South America. Here, they found Indians living in homes built on stilts in the shallow lake of Maracaibo. The Indians used canoes similar to Italian gondolas to get to the main land. These scenes reminded the Spaniards of Venice, Italy, so they called the area "Litte Venice" or Venezuela.

These Spaniards eventually took control of the entire regions of Peru, Ecuador and Columbia. Spanish Conquestadors followed in the 16th century in search of Indian treasure and gold. In the early 1800's, a young Venezuelan named Simon Bolivar vowed to free his native country and the other colonies from Spanish rule. He led armies, that in time, liberated several colonies including Bolivia, which is named after him. Independence came to Venezuela in 1830.

The Venezuelan countryside is not suited well for agriculture. Coffee and sugar cane are about the only crops grown for export. The lowlands tend to be too wet one-half of the year and too hot and dry the other half.

Only a few decades ago, oil was discovered in Venezuela. Oil wells sprang up everywhere, but especially in and around Lake Maracaibo and the Gulf of Venezuela. Several international oil companies now have huge operations there. The country soon became one of the leading oil producing and exporting nations of the world. The cities around the lake and the capital city of Caracas became showplaces for hotels, highrises and highways. However, the hillsides around these cities continue to shelter the majority of the people in poor living conditions.

In the southeastern portion of Venezuela lies the delta region of the Orinoco River. Here dense forests and jungles are home to a variety of animals, including monkeys, boa constrictors, alligators and the world's largest rodent, the hundred pound "capybara."

Venezuela is a combination of wealthy, modern cities, uninhabitable jungles and plains and poverty-stricken villages.

Interesting Facts:

● Venezuela is probably the wealthiest country in South America, but, only 3% of it's people control 90% of it's land and resources.

● The highest waterfall in the world is Angel Falls in Venezuela. The water falls 3,212 feet (979 meters) or 15 times higher than Niagara Falls. It was discovered in 1935, by an American aviator, Jimmy Angel, while searching for gold.

● The ancient Inca Indians were highly skilled in farming and engineering. They built elaborate roads, developed farming techniques and made beautiful ornaments of gold and silver. When the Spaniards conquered the Inca empire, the Inca treasure was melted down and sent back to Spain.

Important Holidays:

● Venezuela Independence Day is June 5th. This national holiday commemorates the country's independence from Spain in 1811.

● The birthdate of Simon Bolivar is celebrated on July 24th, in Venezuela. It is a national holiday complete with parades and picnics.

● From December 16 through 24, many churches hold a daily, early morning "Christmas Carol Mass" or Misa de Aguinaldo. In the capital of Caracas, neighborhoods hold parties and at bedtime children tie a string to their big toes and let the ends hang out the windows. The next morning, friends pull the strings to wake the children up.

Famous People:

● Simon Bolivar, "The Liberator," a South American revolutionary and statesman was born in 1783. He was only 22 years old when he began his move to free his country from Spanish rule.

Some Things To Do:

● Ask your students to locate local monuments or buildings that they can compare to the height of Angel Falls. (The Sears Tower in Chicago, is only 1,454 feet tall.)

● Have your students investigate the destruction of the Rain Forests of South America. What can they do to help?

● Bring in some raw sugar cane for your students to sample.

Venezuela

Venezuela

The Flag of Venezuela

South East Asia

Cambodia - Also known as "Kampuchea" after a communist revolution in 1975, this beautiful country was once the great empire of the Khmer people.

Laos - Once part of French Indo-China, Laos has no seacoasts or railroads and few roads. Most of the people live in small villages along the Mekong River.

Philippines - This large group of islands is south of China and east of Vietnam. Until 1898, it was ruled by the Spanish and then ceded to the U.S.A. It is now an independent country.

Thailand - Until a military revolt in 1991, this fascinating country had always been independent with a king as its leader. The country was originally called Siam.

Vietnam - The North and South were united into one country in 1976 after many years of fighting. Most of the people live in the large cities of Hanoi or Ho Chi Minh City (Saigon.)

There are several countries and many islands in South East Asia, most of which are covered in thick tropical forests and have very heavy rainfall for part of the year. In these forests such trees as teak and mahogany are cut down for their beautiful wood. It is not unusual to see elephants carrying huge logs from the jungle. This area of the world also provides a very important food crop - Rice. Rice grows well in wet, hot countries. The hillsides are terraced by hand to allow the best possible conditions to grow the rice. If the rainy season is especially long, farmers can grow two crops of rice a year.

Since water is so important to the lives of South East Asians, it is natural that some people simply live their entire lives on the water. The Bajau people do just that! The Bajaus live on wooden boats and sail between and throughout the islands and the mainland of all South East Asia. Their boats are called "lipas." Most Bajau families cook, eat and sleep on the boats. The walls and roofs of the boats are made of woven mats which provide shade in the hot sun. They eat mainly a vegetable root called "cassava" which they buy from islanders and fish which they catch. They cook with a fire contained in an earthen pot so the wooden boat is safe from burning. Some Bajaus live in houses built on stilts near the coasts or along rivers. Children often walk on stilts through the shallow water to get from one house to another.

At one time, the countries of Vietnam, Laos and Cambodia were called French Indo-China. The French withdrew in 1954. Vietnam was divided into two parts, causing a long civil war to develop. South Vietnam fell to the communist North in 1975 and Vietnam became united as a Communist Republic. Struggles continue for the people of these countries in their fight for democratic freedom.

Interesting Facts:

- Laos is known as "The Land of a Million Elephants."

- For hundreds of years an ancient temple known as Angkor Wat was hidden in the jungles of Cambodia. Once uncovered, massive temples, gates, canals and carvings were found. It was built by the Khmers during the Khmer Empire. No one knows why it was abandoned.

- The Philippines is the only country in Asia which is mostly Christian. The prominent religion in South East Asia is Buddhism.

- During the wet season, Cambodia's "Tonle Sap," the "Great Lake" triples its normal size.

- The name Thailand means "free nation."

Important Holidays:

- "Songkran", in Thailand, is celebrated in mid April. This New Year celebration takes place during the hottest time of the year. People squirt water at one another, even strangers. It's a blessing to get wet because it is believed that the water washes away evil. People often release birds from cages and pour fish from their bowls into rivers as a symbol of good deeds.

- "Pista Ng Anihan" is celebrated on May 15 in the Philippines. "Pista" comes from the Spanish word "fiesta." People decorate their homes, typically showing their professions, and join neighbors in playing sports in gratitude of a plentiful harvest.

- "Tet-Trung-Thu", (Mid-Autumn Festival) is celebrated in Vietnam around September 15. People carry colorful lanterns during evening festivities. Moon cakes, round, flat cakes filled with sweetened black beans, are a special treat during the celebrations.

Important People:

- Ho Chi Minh, 1890-1969, president of the Democratic Republic of Vietnam, (North Vietnam.)

- Ferdinand Marcos, president of the Philippines from 1965-73.

- Lon Nol, leader of Cambodia 1970-75, declared Cambodia a republic.

- Nguyen Van Thieu, president of South Vietnam 1965-75.

Some Things To Do:

- Ask your students to make brightly colored, paper lanterns to celebrate "Tet-Trung-Thu."

- Have your students each decorate their desk, illustrating their hobbies or interests in celebration of "Pista Ng Anihan."

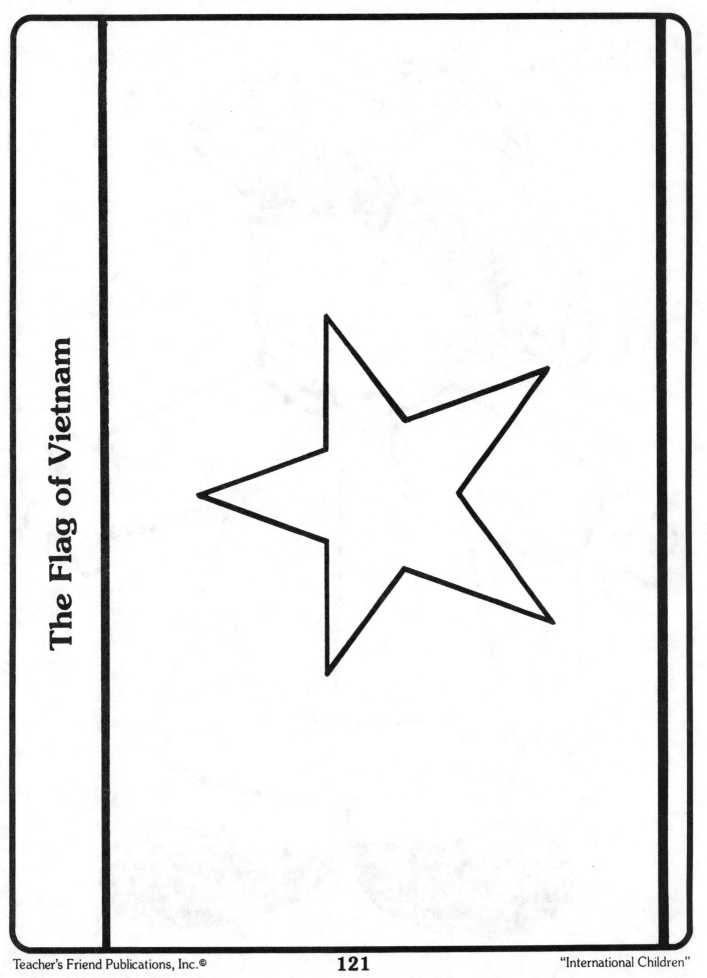

The Flag of Vietnam

Vietnam

Vietnam

South Korea

Capital City: Seoul

Main Language: Korean

Currency: Won

Area: 38,000 sq. mi. (98,400 sq. km.)

Population: 42,000,000

Main Religions: Taoism, Buddhist, Confucian, Christian

Government: Constitutional Republic

People: Koreans

Flag: A red and blue circle showing the Chinese symbols of yin and yang is placed in the center of a white field. In each corner of the flag is a set of three black bars, representing divination.

Korea is one of the world's oldest nations. For many years, Korea was called the "Hermit Kingdom" because no one knew very much about it. During this time, Koreans did not want visitors. They kept very much to themselves.

In the late 19th and early 20th centuries, westerners entered Korea as missionaries and traders. At that time, Japan, China and Russia were fighting for control of northeast Asia. In 1910, Japan was victorious and occupied Korea. Korea remained under Japanese control until the end of World War II, in 1945. After World War II in 1950, North Korea, (under communist control) invaded South Korea. It was their goal to unite the country under communism. The Korean War followed. A treaty was signed in 1953, but the country is still divided today -- two countries, North Korea and South Korea. The dividing line is known as the 38th parallel.

Most of Korea is covered by mountains. Because it is so mountainous, only about 22% of the land can be farmed. Instead of agriculture, Korea has developed other industries. Today, South Korea produces much of the clothing worn in the United States. Factories produce a flood of modern things, from tennis shoes to home appliances.

The capital of South Korea is Seoul, which means "capital." It is also the center of business and culture. Today, Seoul is a very modern city but its history goes back hundreds of years. The ancient Kyongbokung Palace of the Yi Dynasty houses a national museum. The 1988 Summer Olympics were held in the city of Seoul.

Important Facts:

● The Korean word for family home is "chip."

● Korea is about the size of the state of Utah. It is so hilly, however, that some people have said that if the mountains could be ironed out the country would be larger than the state of Texas.

● Most Koreans, today, have three names. The first is the family name, the second a generation name and the third is a chosen name. Long ago, girls received only their father's name and were called his daughter.

● In Korea, people show respect for each other by bowing. A very respectful bow is one in which a person puts their knees and hands flat on the ground. They then bow forward, their forehead touching their hands.

Important Holidays:

● New Year's Celebrations, January 1-3, is the largest Korean holiday. Ancient Koreans told their children that if they fell asleep on the last night of the year their eyebrows would turn white. Today, just for fun, older children put white flour on the eyebrows of their younger brothers and sisters while they sleep.

● Urini Nal, May 5th, is Korean Children's Day. On this day, parents take their children to puppet shows and play games with them. It is believed that children deserve one day of their own in return for the obedience they are expected to give all year.

● Hangul Nal, October 9, is Alphabet Day. In 1446, King Sejong the Great proclaimed a new alphabet to be used in Korea. Today, calligraphy contests are held and prizes given.

Important People:

● King Sejong ruled Korea from 1419 to 1450. He gave his people a new way of writing called "Han'gul."

● Admiral Yi Sun-sin, stopped the Japanese invasion of his country in 1592.

● Non'gae was a woman who resisted the Japanese in 1592. Her memory is honored on a stone called the "Rock of Faithful Women."

Some Things To Do:

● The game "Paper, Scissors, Rock" came from Korea and is called "kawi bawi bo." Play this game with a friend.

● The greeting "yobo" is used in a variety of ways depending upon who you are addressing. "Yobosipsio" would be used to address your teacher. "Yoboseyo" would be used to address friends and strangers. Just using the greeting "yobo" is the least polite form. Practice greeting people using these Korean words.

South Korea

The Flag of South Korea